The Deerhound

Vintage Dog Books
Home Farm
44 Evesham Road
Cookhill, Alcester
Warwickshire
B49 5LJ

www.vintagedogbooks.com

©Vintage Dog Books 2007
This book is copyright and may not be
reproduced or copied in any way without
the express permission of the publisher in writing

ISBN No. 978-1-4067-8775-7

British Library Cataloguing-in-publication Data
A catalogue record for this book is available
from the British Library.

Vintage Dog Books
Home Farm
44 Evesham Road
Cookhill, Alcester
Warwickshire
B49 5lJ

www.vintagedogbooks.com

THE DEERHOUND.

FAILING any further information on the subject than we at present possess, it will always be a moot point whether the hounds used for Queen Elizabeth's delectation at Cowdray Park, in 1595, that "pulled down sixteen bucks in a laund," were the ordinary greyhounds or the Scottish deerhounds. The latter were likely enough to be fashionable animals at the close of the sixteenth century, for they had already been described by Boece, in his History of Scotland, published in 1526; and, thirty-four years later, Gesner, in his "General History of Quadrupeds," gives an illustration of three Scottish dogs, one of them answering to our modern deerhound in general appearance. The drawing for this was supplied by Henry St. Clair, Dean of Glasgow at that time, whose family kept the breed for very many years, an interesting story in connection therewith being told on another page.

Good Queen Bess was fond of her dogs and the

sport they showed, and there is nothing unreasonable in supposing that those provided for the purpose above mentioned at Cowdray were in reality deerhounds. However, whether my supposition be correct or otherwise, there is no gainsaying the fact that this mention in the Scottish history is the earliest I have met with where the deerhound is actually alluded to.

Later on he became popular enough, and that he was highly valued by the clans or chieftains of his native country may be judged from the following story given by Raphael Holinshead, whose "Chronicles" were published about 1577. He says that many of the Pictish nobility repaired to Craithlint, to meet the King of Scots to hunt and make merry with him, where they found the Scottish dogs far excelled their own in "fairness, swiftness, and hardness, and also in long standing up and holding out." The Scottish lords gave their guests both dogs and bitches of their best strains; but they, not contented, stole one belonging to the king from his keeper; and this the most esteemed hound in the lot. The master of the leash being informed of the robbery, pursuit was taken after the thievish Picts, who, being overtaken, refused to give up the royal favourite, and in the end slew the master of the leash with their spears. Then the Scots mustered a

The Deerhound.

stronger force, including those who had been engaged in hunting, and they fell upon the Picts. A terrible struggle took place, one hundred of the Picts were slain and "threescore gentlemen" on the other side, besides a great number of commoners. The latter, poor fellows, not being deemed worthy of numeration in those bloodthirsty times, and, so long as the hound was recovered, little thought would be given to the dead "commoners" who fought for its possession, and, it is stated, few of them ever knew what the fight had been about.

Another interesting story is that relating to the family of St. Clair. King Robert Bruce, in following the chase upon the Pentland Hills, had often started a "white faunch deer," which always escaped from his hounds. He asked his nobles if any of them possessed dogs that they thought might prove more successful. Naturally, there was no one there so bold as to affirm his hounds better than those of the sovereign, until Sir William St. Clair came forward. He would wager his head that his two favourite hounds, "Help," and "Hold," would kill the deer before she could cross the March burn. Bruce, evidently of a sporting turn, at once wagered the Forest of Pentland Moor, to the head of the bold Sir William, against the accomplishment of the feat. The deer was roused by the slow, or drag hounds, and St. Clair, in a suitable place, uncoupled his favourites in sight of the flying deer. St. Clair followed on horseback, and as the deer reached the middle of the brook, he in despair, believing his wager already lost, and his life as good as gone, leaped from his horse. At this critical moment, "Hold" stopped her quarry in the brook, and "Help" coming up, the deer was turned, and in the end killed within the stipulated boundary. The king, not far behind, was soon on the scene, and embracing his subject, " bestowed on him the lands of Kirton, Logan House, Earncraig, &c., in free forestrie." Scrope says the tomb of this Sir William Clair, on which he appears sculptured in armour, with a greyhound (deerhound) at his feet, is still to be seen in Rosslyn Chapel.

Thomson Gray in his "Dogs of Scotland" (1890), tells us that the earliest mention of deerhounds appears in 1528, in Pitcott's History of that country, wherein it is stated that "the king desired all gentlemen that had dogs that were good, to bring them to hunt in the said boundaries, which most of the noblemen of the Highlands did, such as the Earls of Huntley, Argyle, and Athole, who brought their deerhounds with them, and hunted with His Majesty.

However, about this time, and for many years later, a common but erroneous idea prevailed, that

The Deerhound.

the Irish wolfhound and the Scottish deerhound, were identical, and indeed, that the latter was merely an ordinary greyhound, with a rough, hard coat, produced by beneficent Nature to protect a delicate dog against the rigours of a northern climate.

About the end of the sixteenth century (1591), we are told that the Earl of Mar had large numbers of these deerhounds, but at the same period the Duke of Buckingham had great difficulty in obtaining Irish wolf dogs, a few couples of which, he wished to present to "divers princes and other nobles." So the Irish dog was even then becoming extinct, but the Scottish one, though rarer later on, survives to the present day, and is now more popular and numerous than at any previous period of his existence. Still, judging from what Pennant, writing in 1769, says, the deerhound must, about his time, have been in danger of extinction, for he says, "he saw at Gordon Castle, a true Highland greyhound, which has become very scarce. It was of large size, strong, deep chested, and covered with very long and rough hair. This kind was in great vogue in former days, and used in vast numbers at the magnificent stag chases by powerful chieftains."

One or two authors have assumed that the modern deerhound is a cross between the foxhound and the greyhound, or between the bloodhound and the greyhound, but this I consider quite incorrect, nor in my researches have I been able to come across anything likely to sustain such a statement. If the deerhound is to be found in greater numbers now than previously, it is only because more attention is paid to his breeding, and because the many strains that a hundred years and more ago were in the out of the way places of the Highlands have, by better communication, been brought within the radius of canine admirers. Scrope, in his "Deer Stalking," published in 1838, has naturally much to write about the deerhound. He it is recommends the foxhound and greyhound cross, and says that the celebrated sportsman Glengarry crossed occasionally with bloodhound, still Macneill of Colonsay, who wrote the article in "Days of Deerstalking," that deals mostly with those hounds, confesses that there were still pure deerhounds to be found when he states them to be very scarce at the time he wrote. Maybe they were scarce, but not sufficiently so as to induce people to attempt to reproduce them by such an unhallowed alliance.

A favourite sporting author from my earliest boyhood days has been Charles St. John, who, in his "Highland Sports," writes so charmingly and naturally of all he saw and shot and caught during his excursions. He wrote but eight years after Scrope,

The Deerhound.

still he says that the breed of Deerhounds which "had nearly become extinct, or, at any rate, was very rare a few years ago, has now become comparatively plentiful in all the Highland districts, owing to the increased extent of the preserved forests and the trouble taken by different proprietors and masters of mountain shootings who have collected and bred this noble race of dogs regardless of expense and difficulty." Not a word about Macneill's crosses or of those of Glengarry; and I am happy in the belief that our present race of deerhounds does not contain the slightest taint of bloodhound or foxhound blood for over a century. If it did, surely the black and tan colour and the greyhound markings would continually be appearing. I have yet to see a black and tan deerhound, or one similar to a foxhound in hue.

What an excellent picture St. John draws of Malcolm: "as fine a looking lad, of thirty-five, as ever stepped on heather," and of his two hounds, Bran and Oscar, whose descriptions tally with what I shall later on give to be those of a deerhound. There were no bloodhound and foxhound in Bran or Oscar, and well might such handsome, useful, faithful creatures, or similar ones, be worth the £50 a-piece, they would have brought even forty-five years ago.

Since St. John wrote some deer forests have been broken up into smaller holdings, and to this, perhaps, may be attributed the fact that "coursing deer" is not followed so much as in his time. There are still some forests in which a deerhound may be taken out to assist at the termination of a stalk; but as the red deer is now mostly killed in "drives," a sort of battue in which the shooter can sit at ease until the deer come by, to be shot in a somewhat ignominious manner, the deerhound as such is little used. A stalker will find one useful at times, but even he is supplied with such a perfect rifle, so admirably sighted, and he is such a crack shot, that the stag seldom requires more than the hard bullet to kill him almost dead upon the spot.

About three years ago, the Earl of Tankerville, in a series of articles he wrote for the *Field*, made allusion to the deerhound. He said some that he saw " were beautiful, swift, and powerful. Some are able to pull down a stag single handed, but the bravest always gets killed in the end. The pure breed have keen noses as well as speed, and will follow the slot of a wounded deer perseveringly if they find blood. The most valued are not necessarily the most savage, for the latter (the reckless ones) go in and get killed, whilst the more wary, who have taken the hint after a pug or two, are equally enduring, and will hold their bay for any indefinite time, which is a merit of the first importance."

The Deerhound.

Lord Tankerville continues, that he was informed of a remarkable deerhound, belonging to a poacher in Badenoch, that never missed a deer. In due course he obtained the hound, and called it Bran. Later on it saved the life of a keeper from the furious attack of one of the wild bulls of Chillingham. After being delivered to his new home, Bran was placed in the kennel, and it was thought that the pallisades with which it was surrounded were sufficiently high to prevent any dog getting over them. However, Bran did succeed in scaling them, and Lord Tankerville, having paid his money and lost his dog, was considerably upset, and never thought of seeing the hound again. However, in a few days the "poacher" brought back the errant Bran, who had, in fact, reached his old home before his master, who was considerably astonished, on reaching his cottage, to see his old companion rush forward to meet him. The distance between Chillingham and the man's cottage was about seventy miles, and, to take the shortest route, which Bran no doubt did or he would have caught his master on the road, he must have swum Loch Ericht.

No doubt modern dog shows have done much to re-popularise the deerhound, now that he is so seldom used for that purpose for which, shall I say, nature first intended him. How little he is used in deer stalking may be surmised by a list that appears in Mr. Weston Bell's monograph of the variety (1892). Here some fifty-eight forests are named, and in but about seven of them is the deerhound kept. The collie is now more frequently trained and used to track the wounded stag, because he works more slowly, and is therefore less liable to unduly scare and alarm the deer. From the earliest institution of dog shows, classes have been provided for the deerhound, and these have resulted in a number of excellent animals being benched of a uniformity and quality that our excellent friend Charles St. John would scarcely have thought possible, and Mr. M'Neil would have deemed an impossibility.

There is no handsomer dog than the deerhound— he has the elegance of shape, the light airy appearance of the greyhound, a hard, crisp, and picturesque jacket, either of fawn or grey brindle, an eye as bright as that of the gazelle, but loving, still sharp and intelligent; and a good specimen has not a bad feature about him. His disposition is of the best; he is sensible and kindly; and friends of mine to whom I gave a puppy, on its death refused to be consoled by any other dog than one of the same variety.

"It's a blooming lurcher," is the yokel's idea of a deerhound, an opinion in which the cockney corner man evidently coincides. Either will pass a rude

The Deerhound.

remark about your aristocratic canine companion. The Scotchman away from home, be he out at elbows, or otherwise, pays compliments to the dog. If his shoes are down at the heels the chances are he is the remains of a chieftain of some great clan, and, on the strength of your possession of one of his native quadrupeds, will seek to allay his thirst, or penchant for Glenlivat, at your expense. Still, I do not fancy that the deerhound is quite so popular as a companion over the border as he is on this side the border. Englishmen have paid greater attention to his breeding; the honours to be gained at shows make it worth while their doing so; and, being more difficult to rear than most other dogs, he requires greater care in bringing up, and, if not allowed continual exercise, will become crooked on his fore legs, and out at the elbows—ungainly enough in little dogs, but a terrible eyesore in big ones. They will not rear well in a kennel.

It has been said the deerhound is uncertain in his temper with children; in some cases this may be so, but not in all. Again, it has been stated that when a puppy he will chase anything that moves in front of him—sheep, poultry, &c. What puppy will not? All young dogs are alike in this particular, and if not carefully watched will, like your favourite little boy or girl, be for ever getting into mischief.

Deerhounds, like all other dogs, require early training, and when once broken off sheep and other "small deer," are as safe and reliable in the fields as any other of the canine race. As a fact, I believe that both pointers and setters, greyhounds, and even the collie himself, is as, "fond of mutton" as the often maligned dog about which this article is being written. Many dogs have been spoiled by their manners being neglected during their puppyhood; no doubt others will be so in the future, and it is a pity that one so docile, handsome, sagacious, and aristocratic as the deerhound, should obtain an evil name through the negligence or over-indulgence of its owner.

As already stated, dog shows have been of infinite advantage in raising the deerhound to its present popularity, though prior to this epoch, what Sir Walter Scott writes of his Maida and other favourite hounds, with Landseer's fine paintings, had made the general public anxious to see such handsome dogs in the flesh. The first show at Birmingham, in 1860, provided two classes for them, but there were few entries, and both leading prizes were taken by Lieut.-Colonel Inge, of Thorpe, near Tamworth, who, at that time, possessed a capital strain of them. Later on the numbers increased, and in 1862 there were ten competitors in the dog class, but they were a mixed lot, though the winner, called Alder, bred by

The Deerhound.

Sir John Macneil, was a splendid specimen, which again took leading honour two years later. The succeeding show had, for some reason or other, a capital entry, sixteen in the one class, six in the other, and these included several dogs from the Highlands, one of the latter, called Oscar, now beating Alder, who looked old and worn, and was past his best.

About this period Lord Henry Bentinck took great pride in his deerhounds, and kept a fine kennel of them. Mr. McKenzie, Ross-shire; Mr. J. Wright, Yeldersby House, Derby; Mr. Menzies, Cherthill; Mr. Grant, Glenmorriston; Colonel Campbell of Monzie; Lord Boswell; Mr. W. Gordon, Guardbridge, Fifeshire; Lord Bredalbane; the Duke of Sutherland; Mr. Spencer Lucy, and Dr. Hadden, have all at one time or another had good deerhounds in their kennels, as well as many of the older Scottish families.

In 1871 we find a Cameron of Lochiel sending to Curzon Hall and taking a first prize with Bruce. Sir St. George Gore was a frequent exhibitor, and in 1865 he showed a deerhound that was quite smooth, a big coarse, ugly greyhound in appearance, that of course did not take a prize. Mr. H. C. Musters, Captain Graham, of Durnock, and a few others who admired the fine form of the Scotch dog, were exhibiting about 1870. The following year had the celebrated Warrior, that won so many prizes up and down the country, mostly in variety classes. However, prior to him came one or two exceptionally good dogs, Mr Beasley's bitch Countess especially so; nor must Mr. Hickman's excellent bitch Morna be omitted, for he was not only good to look at, but could boast a lineage which contained some of the bluest blood of the day. Following a few years later was that fine old dog Bevis (Mr. Hood Wright's), so sober and sedate that in his declining years he took to the stage, and appeared with great success at one or two of the Sheffield pantomimes at Christmas.

There are now, at least a dozen shows held annually, at which classes are provided for this variety, and naturally new breeders have sprung up. Mr. E. Weston Bell, of Rossie, Perthshire, has got together a kennel containing a number of splendid deerhounds; and Mr. W. H. Singer, of Frome, Somerset; Mr. Walter Evans, Birchfield, Birmingham; Mr. R. H. Wright, Newton-le-Willows; Mr. H. P. Parker, Stourbridge; Mr. W. Gibbons, Stratford-on-Avon; Mr. A. Maxwell, Croft, near Darlington; Major Lewis, Bath, all possess deerhounds of the highest merit. Perhaps the best of the race, at the time I write, in the summer of

The Deerhound.

1892, are Sir Gavin, Fingall II., Earl II., Ensign, Shepherd, Swift, Enterprise, Royal Lufra (a beautiful headed bitch, for which excellence she won a special prize at Bath not long ago), Rossie Blue Bell, and there are many others, almost, if not equally good to look at on the show bench.

The deerhound, in colour, should be either brindled in various shades, blue, or fawn; white is detrimental, though a little on the chest or feet does not matter very much. Pure white dogs are occasionally found, but it is not a deerhound colour, any more than it is that of a collie, though Mr. Morton Campbell, jun., of Stracathro, near Brechin, has a white hound of considerable beauty, and though obtained from the Highlands, its pedigree is unknown. I prefer the darker shades of colour; the darker brindles are very attractive, and in actual work, it is a colour that tones well with the surrounding rocks and dark heather. The largest and heaviest dogs are not to be recommended, either for work or otherwise, they cut themselves on the rocks, and are not nearly so active and lithe on the rough ground as the lighter and smaller specimens. The dog should not, at any rate, be more than about thirty inches at the shoulder, the bitch from one to two inches less. One or two specimens have been shown, and won prizes too, that measured up to thirty-two inches, and even an inch more, and it is said that Bran, figured in "Dogs of the British Isles," was thirty-three inches! Such are too big for work, and nowadays have not much chance of winning on the show bench. The following heights and weights of some of the best deerhounds of the modern standard may be interesting, and all are excellent specimens in every way, and perhaps equal to anything that has yet been seen. Mr. Walter Evan's Fingal II., stands $29\frac{3}{4}$ inches at shoulder, and weighs 87lb.; his Earl II., $28\frac{3}{4}$ inches and 81lb.; Duke of Brewood, $30\frac{1}{4}$ inches, weighs 88lb.; and his bitch, Enterprise, stands 29 inches, and weighs 85lb., a big weight for a bitch. Mr. W. H. Singer's well-known dog, Swift, is 79lb. weight, and 30 inches at the shoulder; and his bitch, She, weighs 72lb., and stands $26\frac{1}{2}$ inches.

In general form the deerhound should be like a greyhound: ears similar, loins likewise, legs and feet equally good. In his character he differs from the smooth hound considerably, as he does in coat, which is hard, crisp, and close, not too long, and silkiness on the top knot, and elsewhere, is not desirable. In running he carries his head higher than a greyhound, nor does he lay himself down so closely to his work; in galloping, he appears to be on the look out for contingencies, and does not, as a rule, go at

The Deerhound.

his greatest pace, unless actually required to do so. He hangs back, as it were—maybe to avoid a stroke from the stag, or to look out for the proper place to seize; some will seize one part, some another. "Bran's point of attack was always at the shoulder or fore leg, whilst Oscar had a habit of biting at the hind leg, above the hock, frequently cutting through the flesh and tendons in an extraordinary manner, and tumbling over the deer very quickly," says St. John in his "Highland Sports."

Their endurance is great, their scent keen, and Ronaldson Macdonnel, of Glengarry, instances one dog, that, held in a leash, followed the track of a wounded stag, in unfavourable rainy weather, for three successive days, when the game was shot. The story goes, that this stag was wounded within three miles of Invergarry House, and was traced that night to the Glenmoriston. At dusk, in the evening, the stalkers placed a stone on each side of the last fresh print of his hoof, and another over it; and this they did each night following. On the succeeding morning they removed the upper stone, when the dog recovered the scent, and the deer was that day hunted over a great part of the Glenmoriston ground. On the third day, it was retraced on to Glengarry, and there shot.

When hunting, the deerhound runs mute, as he

does when coursing, but when the stag is brought to bay, the hound opens, and by his "baying," or barking, attracts his master to the spot, where, in some pool, with a steep rock at his back, the noble monarch of the glen in vain bids defiance to his foes.

In puppyhood, the deerhound is delicate, and difficult to rear, that scourge known as distemper carrying off large numbers. This is, no doubt, owing to continued inbreeding, but with our increasing knowledge of canine ailments, the mortality is decreasing.

During 1892, a club for looking after the welfare of the deerhound was formed, but at the time I write, their description of the dog has not been published. They, however, have decided not to give any numerical list of points. Failing the club's standard, I have carefully compiled the following description:

The deerhound is an elegantly shaped, graceful dog, a good specimen being almost perfect in symmetry. He should be particularly neat and cleanly cut about the neck and shoulders, perfectly straight in front, stifles well turned behind, and generally giving the appearance of speed and power, with freedom in his movements. His face and eyes are pleasing in their expression, bright in their intelli-

The Deerhound.

gence—a perfect deerhound is perhaps about the most sensible looking of all our dogs, not even excepting the collie.

In *head* and *face* the deerhound is not unlike a rather rough-headed greyhound, perhaps wider in skull and stronger in jaw and nose, and the shaggy brow and more hairy face give him a hardier and less polished appearance. The head should have the greatest width at the ears, and taper gradually to the nose, without any dip between the eyes. The jaws should be level and very powerful.

The *eyes* ought to be bright, dark, or hazel, sparkling, not too big, but just big enough; beaming with intelligence and good nature, and from which he obtains, in a great degree, his charming expression. Light coloured eyes are condemned.

Ears small, soft, glossy, free from long hair, and should be darker coloured than the rest of the body. A little silky hair on the ears is often seen in good specimens. When excited the ear is raised high, without quite losing the fold, not quite a semi-prick ear.

Neck long, strong and muscular, gracefully poised, quite as long as that of the greyhound; but the "mane," which a good coated dog ought to have, makes the neck look short.

The *chest* and *shoulders* are important, and the former must be deep, but not wide in front; ribs fairly well sprung, and the shoulders neatly and elegantly laid, for if too upright the hound is sure to be slow.

Back and *loins* strong and very powerful, the latter firm and hard; back not level, but rather arched towards the loins, for the same reason a greyhound is similarly shaped.

Legs and *feet:* The former must be straight in front, strong and muscular, and without any undue heaviness near the shoulder that is likely to give an appearance of being out at the elbows. Hind legs particularly well muscled, stifles strong and neatly turned, so displaying the "sickle hocks." Stiffness or stiltiness in the hind quarters ought to be absolute disqualification, for a deerhound that cannot gallop, and walks like a dancing master, is of no use whatever; feet firm, thick, well arched, with the toes close and strong.

The *coat* should be hard, crisp and close, without any degree of softness or woolliness—the latter is very bad. One inclined to be curly and crisp and hard and dense is to be preferred to a perfectly straight jacket that is soft, fine, and open. Silkiness or softness of the hair on the skull is to be guarded against, though it repeatedly appears; indeed, most specimens are silkier here than on other parts of the body. There should be a hard close coat down the

The Deerhound.

legs in accordance with the quantity carried by the dog elsewhere, though nothing approaching feather. The typical deerhound ought to have a fairly coated head, and a good, moderately long and hard jacket all over, but not a profuse or shaggy one.

Colour: Dark brindled, fawn brindled, and fawn are the best colours; white deerhounds are sometimes seen, but are not to be encouraged, and no doubt the brindles in their varying shades are the most fashionable and the best colours. Fawns not too red and fawns of a lighter shade are not so frequently met with; both are good, and in the judging ring are equal to the brindles. Blues or slate coloured hounds are likewise repeatedly seen, though not so common now as some years ago, and this colour is quite equal to either the fawns or brindles. A little white on the breast or on the feet is not detrimental, but a deerhound is a "whole coloured" dog, and patched or gaudily marked puppies ought to be destroyed when born. All very light coloured dogs should have black points. As to puppies, although black and tan is not allowable in a full grown dog, Mr. Hickman tells me that his well-known grey-blue bitch Morna, when a few weeks old, was a perfect black and tan or black, blue and tan, with the tan spots over the eyes, but when her coat changed she became a grey or blue-grizzle in colour.

The *stern* is carried low but gracefully, is full long in proportion to the size of the dog, and should not be smooth, but covered with hair according to the proportion carried by the dog elsewhere. Feathering here, as on the legs, is objectionable.

General Symmetry is an important consideration —by it is to be understood a hound of perfect proportion with all points duly balanced.

Weight, dogs about 85lb. to 105lb.; bitches, about 65lb. to 85lb.

	Value.		Value.
Head and skull	15	Legs and feet	10
Eyes and ears	10	Coat	8
Neck and chest	10	Stern	5
Body, including loins	10	Colour	5
Thighs and hocks	12	General symmetry	15
	57		43

Grand Total **100.**

MR. SPACKMAN'S WINNING COUPLE
A scene in the judging ring at Wissahickon Show

LORD OF THE ISLES
An ideal picture of one of the best dogs owned by Mr. G. W. Hickman, Solihull, England

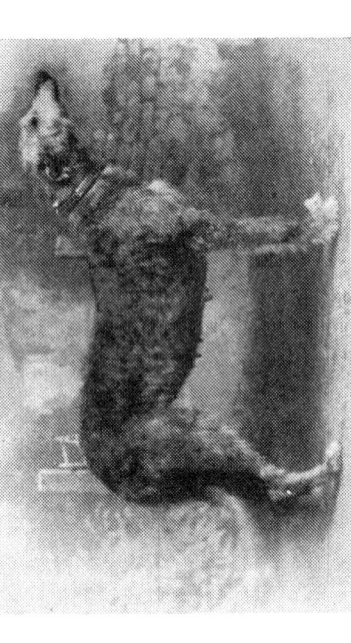

OLGA
The property of Mr. A. L. Page, of New York

DUNROBIN
Bred by the Duke of Sutherland. Late the property of Mr. A. L. Page, of New York

The Scotch Deerhound

F a clear line of descent could be established to the Irish wolfhound precedence would be given to that dog as the oldest type of hunting dog preserved in its original purity, but such not being the case the off-shoot therefrom, the deerhound of Scotland, is entitled to priority. It is a little more than singular that modern writers on the two breeds have contented themselves with the surmise that they were possibly of similar origin, when the fact of their having been the same could have been authenticated so readily. There is a question as to whether there were not two Irish wolfhounds a smooth and a rough, but that there was a rough is not contraverted and it was this rough dog which was also kept in the Highlands of Scotland and has been preserved to this day, not in what we should call original purity, but with his original appearance and characteristics.

The first descriptive reference to these dogs is found in Taylor's "Pennilesse Pilgrimage," published in 1618, and is given in the account of one of the great red-deer hunts of the Earl of Mar. " The manner of the hunting is this: five or six hundred men doe rise early in the morning and they doe disperse themselves various ways, and seven, eight or even ten miles compass they doe bring or chase the deer in many heards (two, three or four hundred in a heard) to such or such a place, as the nobleman shall appoint them. Then when the day is come, the Lords and gentlemen of their companies doe ride or go to the said places, sometimes wading up to their middles through bournes and rivers, and then they being come to the place, doe lye down on the ground till these foresaid scouts, which are called the tinckell, doe bring down the deer; but as the proverb says of a bad cook, so tinckell men doe lick their own fingers, for besides their bows and arrows which they carry with them we can hear now and then a harquebusse going off, which they doe seldom discharge in vain; then after we had stayed three houres or there abouts, we might perceive the deer appear in the hills round about us (their heads making a show like a wood), which

The Dog Book

being followed close by the tinckell, are chased down into the valley where wee lay; then all the valley on each side being waylaid with a hundred couple of strong Irish greyhounds, they are let loose as occasion serves upon the heard of deere, that with the dogs, gunnes, arrowes, durks and daggers, in the space of two houres four-score fat deer were slaine, which after were disposed, some one way and some another, twenty or thirty miles; and more than enough left for us to make merry withal at our rendezvous.

" Being come to our lodgings there was much baking, boyling, roasting, and stewing, as if cook ruffian had been there to have scalded the devil in his feathers—the kitchen being always on the side of a banke, many kettles and pots boyling, and many spits turning and winding, with great varietye of cheere, as venison baked, sodden, roast and stu'de; beef, mutton, goates, kid, hares, fish, salmon, pigeons, hens, capons, chickens, partridge, moorcoots, heathcocks, caperkillies and termagants, good ale, sacke, white and claret, tente (or aligant), and most potent *aqua vitæ*. All this, and more than these, we had continually in superfluous abundance, caught by faulconers, fowlers, fishers and brought by my Lord Marr's tenants and purveyors to vitual the camp, which consisted of fourteen or fifteen hundred men and horses."

The quotation is lengthy, but it is worth giving as showing the number of red deer at that time in the Western Highlands of Scotland and the wholesale manner in which they were killed when attacked in this method of driving. The minuteness of the detail carries with it the conviction that the "pilgrim" was very exact in his statements and being a participant at such gatherings he would not use the term "Irish greyhounds" unless he was fully justified in so doing. Whether, if these dogs had been such immense animals as we read about in some old books, the author of this description would have dwelt upon that fact we leave to the opinion of the reader. Our mind was made up long ago that the many claims to gigantic height in the wolfhound are gross exaggerations, to give them a mild term. Goldsmith mentions them as being as large as a calf of a year old and being four feet high. Buffon eclipses Goldsmith entirely when he says that he had only seen one which when sitting down seemed to be five pieds (a pied was $13\frac{1}{2}$ inches) high, and resembled the dog to which is given the name of Great Dane. There is no evidence that these measurements were taped and when we come to reliable data we find that the Irish and Scottish dogs differed but little. The Marquis of Sligo was one of the last to keep any

The Scotch Deerhound

wolfhounds and to pay attention to their breeding. And it was one of his dogs which Aylmer Bourke Lambert, vice-president of the Linnean Society, measured and found to be 10 inches in length of head, "from tip of nose to back part of skull," and "from the toe to top of the fore shoulder" 28½ inches. That is to say a 27-inch dog, standard measure. As Mr. Lambert was not seeking to depreciate the wolfhound we may presume that this was a large dog which he measured. That height would not have been at all uncommon for a Scottish deerhound. Sir Walter Scott's Maida cannot be given as an example of the latter for he was a black and white dog, a cross between a large Pyrenean sheep dog and a deer hound. He was bred by Macdonell of Glengarry, or Glengarry, as he was commonly called, and he made no secret of his introducing the West Indies bloodhound and the dog of the Pyrenees into his kennel "to prevent the degeneracy which results from consanguinity." Maida must have been a very large dog, but we have not found any record of his height. Coming to later times, we have in Dalziel's "British Dogs" a number of measurements of dogs of about 1880, and of the sixteen heights recorded only two were under 27 inches; the others ranging from 27 inches to 32 inches. The contributor of much of the article in "British Dogs" did not believe in the usefulness of large dogs, considering that 28 inches was as tall as a working dog should be. He stated that he had measured the deerhounds at the Birmingham show of 1873 and gives the particulars of seven named ones, two at 26½ inches, three at 27, one at 28 and one at 30½ inches, adding that there were seven dogs over 30 inches and that the second prize was taken by one of 26 inches. This was in the early days of dog shows and before there could have been any of the breeding for size which dog shows cultivated.

The tallest dog we have had here to our knowledge was Mr. John E. Thayer's Chieftain which measured 31 inches, and he was a dog that beat all England and to the best of our recollection was the largest of the deerhounds of his day. Since then Mr. Lee in his "Modern Dogs" mentions one of 32¾ inches at twenty months. Stonehenge also illustrated a deerhound said to be 33 inches in height, but of that there is much doubt.

Height is not at all an essential in a deerhound, in fact if the dog is to be considered as one for work his height should be limited to a size that would keep him a workman and not merely a show poser. We had but the one objection to Chieftain of his being too large and for that reason always preferred his kennel mate, the bitch Wanda, who was 28½ inches. She showed a little more quality, was much better in ears and was every bit as large as one wants in a deerhound bitch. We do not remember whether we ever had them in opposition in the ring, but if we did then Wanda must have won, or condition beat her. We consider 30 inches as much as a deerhound should measure to be of use. It is a breed which should be judged on the lines of a greyhound, symmetry and speed formation being placed over size.

Reference was made to cross-breeding by Glengarry, but his was an exception to the general usage of deerhound breeders in Scotland, at the time these dogs were used exclusively in deer stalking. There were many other kennels where the utmost care was taken to keep the breed pure, and if any cross became necessary it was obtained from other kennels and not by such radical departures as Glengarry resorted to. There were in his days plenty of rough Scottish greyhounds of stout breeding, even if no deerhounds were obtainable.

Several works have treated at length upon the deerhound, the first of which is Scrope's "Deerstalking," and he commended the cross of the foxhound. Colonsay also wrote on the breed, and St. John, in "Highland Sports," gives many interesting anecdotes and sketches in which deerhounds figure. The most pretentious work is Weston Bell's monograph, published in 1892, from which we learn that the breed is no longer in request in deerstalking, his place even then having been usurped by the less demonstrative collie, taught to track the wounded stag.

The deerhound is a dog that really should be popular, but he is not, at least he has always had a small following here. After Mr. Thayer gave up exhibiting, the only person who took any interest in the breed was Mr. Page, who had some hounds from the Duke of Sutherland's kennels, while of late Mr. Spackman of Philadelphia has been about the only exhibitor, and such was the paucity of competition and the ease with which he secured the prefix of champion for his dogs that he became a strong advocate for increased difficulty in securing that coveted title. Exhibitors who think champion titles won too easily should try collies, fox terriers, Irish terriers or some breed like that and they would not complain of easy wins.

The deerhound so closely approaches the greyhound in conformation that the standard of that dog may be taken to apply for all points except the larger size and greater bone of the deerhound, and his coat. The deerhound's coat should be about 3 inches in length and as harsh as possible to the

The Scotch Deerhound

touch, especially along the back and ribs. It is softer on the under part of the body and is shorter on the head than on the body, but it should not be smooth. In order to obtain the correct expression it is especially necessary that the eyebrows should be shaggy and the moustache somewhat long compared with the skull coat. There should be a beard from the lower jaw, and ears should be small, neatly carried like a greyhound, and covered with short hair, darker than the body coat. The English club for this breed gives the weights as from 85 lbs. to 105 lbs. for dogs and from 65 lbs. to 80 lbs. for bitches. This club has also published the following scale of points:

Head and Skull	15	Coat	8
Eyes and Ears	10	Stern	5
Neck and Chest	10	Colour	5
Body, including Loins	10	General symmetry	15
Thighs and Hocks	12	Legs and Feet	10

Total 100

CADER
"A deerhound of pure Glengarry breed, 28 inches high."
From "Stonehenge on the Dog," 1859

"SCOTCH DEER HOUND"
From Jesse's "Anecdotes," 1845

CH. CHIEFTAIN
A celebrity fifteen years ago when Colonel John E. Thayer's kennel was invincible

THE HOUND FAMILY

HOUNDS form a very large section of the dog family, as the term embraces all dogs which follow game either by sight or by scent. Of the former section the leading member of the present time is the greyhound, and has as its consorts the Irish wolfhound, the Scottish deerhound and the Russian wolfhound. To these may be added the later-made breed for racing and rabbit coursing, called the whippet or snap dog. Of the hounds that follow the quarry by scent we have the bloodhound, foxhound, harrier, beagle and basset; and up to a short time ago there was another variety of large foxhound called the staghound or buckhound, which was used in deer hunting, such as the Royal hunt after carted deer, or after wild deer in some of the still remaining sections of England where they were to be found. The Royal buckhounds were given up some years ago and the carted-deer hunts having fallen into disrepute as had the annual cockney Epping Hunt. Staghounds are not a breed of to-day nor, indeed, are harriers to the extent they were. The harrier is the intermediate dog between the foxhound and the beagle and has been interbred at each end, so that we have foxhound-harriers and beagle-harriers; and the old type of true harrier is confined to a very few English hunts and is not in any sense an American breed, though some small foxhounds in Canada are called harriers or "American foxhounds" as the owner pleases.

Lieutenant-Colonel Hamilton Smith, whose researches into the origin of the dog and the individual breeds have never been properly recognised by modern writers, to whom his work seems to have been unknown, devoted much attention to the question of the early hounds. When he wrote regarding ancient dogs researches in Assyria had not progressed so far as they had in Egypt, and he was only aware of one representation of a long-eared dog, the others being erect-eared. He was therefore inclined to the opinion that the greyhound type was the older. Since his day, however, we have had the Layard researches and those of later times and the pendulous-eared dog was the prevailing one in Assyria, according to sculptures and tablets which have been discovered there. A large number of the Egyptian hunting dogs were also drop-eared and any priority which may be claimed as between the greyhound or tracking hound will have to be based upon some other ground than description of ears.

In old Egyptian and Assyrian representations of dogs we have to take into consideration the conventional type, which differed very much. All Assyrian dogs are stout, strong, muscular dogs of what we should call mastiff type. The Egyptian artists, on the other hand depicted their dogs as leggy, light of build and running more to the greyhound type, "weeds" we would be likely to call them. We know that Assyrian dogs were taken to Egypt as gifts and also as tribute, yet these tribute dogs are painted on Egyptian conventional lines, while the same type of dogs by an Assyrian sculptor are made altogether different. We must therefore discard all of them as truly representative, except where we come across radical differences between Egyptian dogs or between dogs of Assyria.

It was Colonel Hamilton Smith's opinion that, although Greek and Roman authors gave tribal names to some sixteen or seventeen hunting dogs there were but two distinct races: one of greyhounds and one of dogs that hunted by scent. One of these tribal names was the Elymaean, which name was claimed by some to have come down through many generations in one form or another till it became the limer, the bloodhound led in leash or liam to track the quarry to its lair or harbour. There seems also to have been a dog of greyhound type that had a similar name, but with an added "m," its mission being to race at the game and pin it by the nose, whereas the bloodhound was not used further than to locate the game and was never off the lead. In the Assyrian sculptures we find hunting dogs on the lead and they are also represented in a similar manner in Egyptian paintings, both erect- and drop-eared, or, as we would characterise them, greyhounds and scenting hounds. There is nothing in which custom is more of an heirloom than in sporting practice and the leading of the greyhounds in slips, taking the brace of setters on lead, or coupling the hounds, might possibly have had its origin a long way farther back than the Assyrian dog on the leash which Layard considered was one of the oldest tablets he had found at Nineveh. It is only about two hundred years since foxhounds were hunted in couples, and all through the old prints and illustrations hounds are shown in couples when led afield, one man taking each couple.

The Hound Family

There is no reason to question the statement that the hounds originated in the Far East and followed the western migration, or accompanied it along the Mediterranean to Spain and to Ireland, likewise across Europe, leaving the Russian wolfhound's ancestors a little farther west than they did those of the Persian greyhound; dropping the Molossian for Greeks to admire and taking more of the same breed as they spread over Europe, to give to Spain the alaunt and to Germany and Denmark the Great Dane. With them came also the tracking hound and the swift racing dog, developed by centuries of breeding for speed till it became what it is to-day: the perfection of lines with but one object in view.

In the very oldest Greek and Latin books, we find that fads of fancy then existed and certain colours were valued more than others, the highest esteemed being the fawn or red with black muzzle, the colour the late Robert Fulton always maintained was the true bulldog colour and known to us as the red smut, or the fallow smut, according to the shade.

Other colours referred to by Xenophon are white, blue, fawn, spotted or striped; and they ranked according to individual fancy, just as they did for many hundreds of years. It was not until about Markham's time that we find authors discrediting colour as a guide to excellence or defect.

How much original relationship existed between the smooth greyhound and the other racing dogs is something which has been taken for granted and not looked into very closely. The Persian and Russian are the same dog, undoubtedly. So also the Irish wolfhound and the Scottish deerhound, while the smooth greyhound differs from the others as they also differ between themselves. Because they are much alike in shape is not to our mind sufficient evidence upon which to say that they are the same dogs changed by climatic influences, as Buffon held. Buffon maintained that a dog taken to a cold country developed in one direction, while a similar dog sent to a warm climate produced something quite different. Size, conformation, and coat were all changed, according to that authority, and he gave the French matin credit for being the progenitor of a large number of breeds upon that supposition. Climate has influence beyond a doubt, but there are other things just as important, one of which is selection. As far back as men knew anything they must have known that the way to get fast dogs was to breed fast dogs together; and if in eight generations it is possible to completely breed out a bulldog cross on a greyhound, as we shall show later on was accomplished, what is to prevent men all over the world taking any

The Dog Book

kind of medium-sized dogs and breeding them into greyhounds in shape, and eventually approaching them in speed? We have an instance to hand in the Irish wolfhound, which was extinct, yet by crossing Danes and deerhounds a dog of the required type was produced in a very few years. Whippets are the production of about thirty years of breeding between terriers of various breeds, crossed with Italian greyhounds and small greyhounds—and what is more symmetrical than a whippet of class?

The very name of greyhound is to our mind proof that this dog was originally a much smaller and very ordinary dog. Efforts have been made to prove that the greyhound was the most highly valued of all the dogs, hence and in keeping therewith a high origin was necessary for the word grey. According to some it was a derivation from Grew or Greek hound; Jesse held that "originally it was most likely grehund and meant the noble, great, or prize hound." Caius held that the origin of the word was "Gradus in latine, in Englishe degree. Because among all dogges these are the most principall, occupying the chiefest places and being absolutely the best of the gentle kinde of houndes." Mr. Baillie Grohman thinks the probable origin was grech or greg, the Celtic for dog, this having been the suggestion of Whitaker in his "History of Manchester." We can see but one solution of the name and that is from grey, a badger.

There was far more badger hunting than hare hunting when England was overrun with forests and uncultivated land, and a small dog for badgers would have earned his name as the badger hound or "grey" hound. Contemporaneous with this dog was the gazehound, which ran by sight, and, as terriers became a more pronounced breed and "grey" hounds found a more useful field of operations, the latter were improved in size and became classed with the gazehound as a sight hunter, eventually crowding out the older name of the coursing dog. That is our solution, and there is no wrenching a person's imagination with the supposition that Latin was the common language of Britain at the early period when this name was adopted.

We find a very similar substitution of name in the scenting hounds. The term harrier has for so long been associated with the sport of hare hunting that it is common belief that the dog got his name from the hare. A study of Caius would have caused some doubt as to that, for he only names the bloodhound and harrier as hounds of scent. The harrier was the universal hunting dog of his day, being used for the fox, hare, wolf, hart, buck, badger, otter, polecat, weasel, and rabbit. They were also used

The Hound Family

for the "lobster," a very old name for the stoat or martin; but this not being known to a French sporting author, he undertook to instruct his fellow countrymen how to catch rabbits by putting a crawfish into the burrows, having first netted all exits. The crawfish was supposed to crawl in till he got to the rabbits and then nip them till they made a bolt into one of the nets. If we did not have the French book with the instructions in we would feel inclined to doubt the truth of this story, to which, if we mistake not, we first saw reference in one of Colonel Thornton's books.

The meaning of harrier was originally to harry, to rouse the game, and had no reference to hares at all, it being more in regard to deer. In an Act of Parliament of one of the Georges this meaning is given to the name harrier, and was ridiculed in a sporting dictionary of about 1800. From the old spelling of the word, or the variety of methods of spelling it, there is ample evidence that the writers made no attempt to connect the dog with the hare. The Duke of York writes of "heirers," and other spellings are hayrers, hayreres, herettoir, heyrettars, herettor, hairetti. It will be noted that four of these spellings have "e" as the first vowel, while at that time the word hare was always spelt with an "a"; the spelling of harrier then began to change, and "a" replaced the "e" as the first vowel, and when harrier became thoroughly established the name eventually became more associated with the hounds specially kept for hare hunting until it was given to no other, and it finally became accepted that the harrier was a dog kept for hare hunting, and presumably always had been. That is something we can trace, but the probable transfer of the name of the badger dog to the hare courser is something that must have taken place years before writing was used to any extent in England.

The old name for running hounds in common use in Europe was brach in one of its many forms. Shakespeare uses the term several times, such as "I had rather hear Lady, my brach, howl in Irish." "Mastiff, greyhound, mongrel grim, hound or spaniel, brach or lym." Mr. Baillie Grohman gives the quotation from "Taming of the Shrew" as follows:—"Huntsman, I charge thee, tender well my hounds, brach Merriman—the poor cur is embossed," but it is now generally held that it should be "trash Merriman—the poor cur is embossed," otherwise, "take care of Merriman, the poor dog is tired out."

Nathaniel Cox, whose "Gentleman's Recreation" went through several editions from 1674 to 1721, gives "rache" as the latest rendering of the word.

The Dog Book

Cox is exceedingly unreliable as an authority, because he copied wholesale from old authors, with only a few alterations of his own. In the quotation referred to he says there were in England and Scotland but "two kinds of hunting dogs, and nowhere else in all the world." These are specified as the rache, with brache as feminine, and the sleuth hound. Here he differs from Caius who gives rache as the Scottish equivalent for the English brache.

Cox copied from some author the statement that the beagle was the gazehound, yet he describes the latter exactly as Caius did, stating that it ran entirely by sight and was "little beholden in hunting to its nose or smelling, but of sharpness of sight altogether, whereof it makes excellent sport with the fox and hare." That most assuredly does not fit the beagle yet a little further on he says, "After all these, the little beagle is attributed to our country; this is the hound which in Latin is called Canis Agaseus, or the Gaze-hound." This is not the agasseus which Oppian states was "Crooked, slender, rugged and full-eyed" and the further description of which fits the Highland terrier much better than the beagle, as we have already set forth in the chapter on the Skye terrier.

Cox credits the greyhound as an introduction from Gaul, but if such was the case they must have been greatly improved in size, or the dogs of the continent must have greatly deteriorated. Quite a number of illustrations of continental greyhounds are available to show the size of the levrier of France and Western Europe, and they all show dogs of the same relative size as those so well drawn in the painting by Teniers of his own kitchen. A hundred years later we have Buffon giving us the height at the withers of the levrier as 15 inches, which is just whippet size.

We have said nothing as to the bloodhound, which is another of those breeds about which there has been a good deal of romance. Originally the bloodhound was the dog lead on leash or liam, variously spelled, to locate the game. An example of the method is shown in the illustration facing page 284, the head and neck of the deer which is being tracked showing very plainly in the thicket close by. The dog having tracked the game to the wood was then taken in a circle around the wood to find whether exit had been made on the other side. If no trace was found the game was then said to be harboured and to this point the huntsmen and hounds repaired later for the hunt. These limers were selected from the regular pack, not on account of any particular breeding, but for their ability to track the slot of the deer, boar, or wolf. This use as slot trackers resulted in the name of

DEERHOUND
By Sir Edwin Landseer

FOXHOUND
By Charles Hancock

GREYHOUND
By A. Cooper

HARRIER
By A. Cooper

BLOODHOUND
By Charles Hancock

BEAGLE
By A. Cooper

TYPICAL HEADS
From the "Sportsman's Annual," 1836

The Hound Family

sleuth hounds being given to them on the Scottish border. Naturally, in the case of wounded animals breaking away and trace of them being lost, these good-nosed dogs found further employment in tracking the quarry by the blood trail, and here we have the bloodhound name. It was ability, not breeding, that caused a dog to be drafted as a limer or bloodhound, and we cannot show this more conclusively, perhaps, than by jumping to the "Sporting Tour" of Colonel Thornton in France in 1802. In describing wild boar hunting he says: "A huntsman sets his bloodhound upon the scent and follows him till he has reared the game." He purchased one of these hounds, which had been bred at Trois Fontaines and illustrated it in his book and it proves to be a basset. Here we have the name applied, as it always had been, to the use the dog was put to and not to the specific breed of the dog. Colonel Thornton, in speaking more particularly of this special dog, said that the breed name was *briquet*.

The prevalent opinion is that the bloodhound is a descendant from what has been called the St. Hubert hound, and in support of this contention the favourite piece of evidence is Sir Walter Scott's lines:

"Two dogs of black St. Hubert's breed,
Unmatched for courage, breath, and speed."

The legend is that in the sixth century, St. Hubert brought black hounds from the South of France to the Ardennes, and it is supposed that these hounds came from the East. It was also said that some white hounds were brought from Constantinople, by pilgrims who had visited Palestine, and on their return they offered these dogs at the shrine of St. Roch, the protecting saint from hydrophobia. These dogs were also called St. Hubert hounds and it is stated that the white dogs were the larger and more prized of the two. The Abbots of St. Hubert gave six hounds annually to the king and it was from these hounds that the best limers were said to be obtained.

If we are to accept later-day poetical descriptions as conclusive evidence, then the St. Hubert hounds were magnificent animals, with all the characteristics of the modern show bloodhound, and with a deep, resounding voice. Records are not made in that fanciful way and what evidence we have is to the effect that the St. Hubert was a heavy, low, short-legged dog, running almost mute and particularly slow in movements. In fact, we are very much of the opinion that the basset is the descendant of the St. Hubert breed. As

The Dog Book

evidence in that direction, we present an extract from that exceedingly scarce work, the "Sportsman's Annual" for 1839. Who the editor was we have not been able to ascertain, but it contains a dozen beautifully executed and coloured dogs' heads drawn specially for this number, seemingly the first of what was to be an annual, but which was only issued the one year. We reproduce a number of the heads of the hounds, by Landseer, Hancock, and Cooper; that of the harrier by the later being, in our opinion, the most beautifully executed head of any dog we have ever seen.

In the letterpress regarding the bloodhound we find the following extract credited to "a small quarto volume of fifteen pages, printed in 1611, and very scarce":

"The hounds which we call St. Hubert's hounds, are commonly all blacke, yet neuertheless, their race is so mingled in these days that we find them of all colours. These are the hounds which the Abbots of St. Hubert haue always kept, or some of their race or kind, in honour or remembrance of the saint, which was a hunter with S. Eustace. Whereupon we may conceiue that (by the Grace of God) all good huntsmen shall follow them into paradise. To returne unto my former purpose, this kind of dogges hath been dispersed through the countries of Henault, Lorayne, Flaunders, and Burgoyne. They are mighty of body, neuertheless their legges are low and short, likewise they are not swift, although they be very good of scent, hunting chaces which are farre stranggled, fearing neither water nor cold and doe more couet the chaces that smell, as foxes, bore, and like, than other, because they find themselues neither of swiftnes nor courage to hunt and kill the chaces that are lighter and swifter. The bloudhounds of this colour proue good, especially those that are cole-blacke, but I make no great account to breede on them or to keepe the kind, and yet I found a booke which a hunter did dedicate to a Prince of Lorayne, which seemed to loue hunting much, wherein was a blason which the same hunter gaue to his bloudhound, called Soullard, which was white, whereupon we may presume that some of the kind proue white sometimes, but they are not of the kind of the Greffiers, or Bouxes, which we haue at these days." The hound Soullyard was a white hound and was a son of a distinguished dog of the same name:

" My name came first from holy Hubert's race,
  Soullyard, my sire, a hound of singular grace."

The Hound Family

The name of the author of the fifteen-page book is, unfortunately, not mentioned, but he was in error regarding the colour of the St. Huberts in the Royal kennels and that of the Greffiers, as he spells the name.

Another importation of hounds was made by St. Louis toward the middle of the thirteenth century, which are described as taller than the usual run of French hounds, and were faster and bolder than the St. Huberts. These were described as *gris de lievre*, which may be interpreted as a red roan. These hounds seem to have been extensively used as a cross on the low French hounds, but no importation seems to have had so much effect as that of the bracco, or bitch, brought from Italy by some scrivener or clerk in the employ of Louis XII. This Italian bitch was crossed with the white St. Huberts and her descendants were known as *chiens griffiers*. So much improvement did these dogs show that special kennels were built for them at St. Germains and they became the popular breed.

Specimens of all of these hounds undoubtedly went to England and we may also assume that English pilgrims and crusaders brought back dogs from the East as they did to France, the progeny of which were drafted as they showed adaptability or were most suited for the various branches of sport, but it is more than doubtful whether any hunting establishments in England approached the greater ones of France. The Duke of Burgundy had in his employ no less than 430 men to care for the dogs and attend to the hunts, hawking and fisheries. There was one grand huntsman, 24 attendant huntsmen, a clerk to the chief, 24 valets, 120 liverymen, 6 pages of the hounds, 6 pages of the greyhounds, 12 under pages, 6 superintendents of the kennels, 6 valets of limers, 6 of greyhounds, 12 of running hounds, 6 of spaniels, 6 of small dogs, 6 of English dogs (probably bulldogs), 6 of Artois dogs; 12 bakers of dogs' bread; 5 wolf hunters, 25 falconers, 1 net-setter for birds, 3 masters of hunting science, 120 liverymen to carry hawks, 12 valets fishermen and 6 trimmers of birds' feathers.

It will be seen, however, that only three varieties of hounds are named, and these were the lines of distinction set by Buffon, who named them levrier, chien courant and basset as the successors of what are named in the foregoing list as greyhounds, running hounds and limers. It is therefore to England we owe the perfection of the greyhound, the preservation of the deerhound, and the improvement and subdivision of the running hounds into foxhounds, harriers and beagles, together with the establishment of type in each variety.

THE DEERHOUND.

BY G. A. GRAHAM, DURSLEY.

THE transition from the Irish Wolfhound to the Deerhound is easy and natural, as in the latter we unmistakably have the descendant of the former. The subject is, moreover, the more easily treated of, as we have many excellent specimens of the Deerhound before us. Indeed, the examples of the breed now scattered in considerable profusion throughout the land are far finer dogs than those of which much boast was made forty years ago.

The earliest records we have of the Deerhound as a distinct breed are, it is believed, given to us by Pennant, who, in his tour in 1769, says:—" I saw also at Castle Gordon a true Highland Greyhound, which has become very scarce. It was of a large size, strong, deep-chested, and covered with very long and rough hair. This kind was in great vogue in former days, and used in vast numbers at the magnificent stag-chases by the powerful chieftains."

Then Macpherson, in his professed translation of Ossian's poems (1773), gives testimony—worthless, no doubt, as regards the Irish Wolfhound, but having a decided value when the Deerhound is considered, as it was almost a certainty that he wrote his descriptions from the living animal. The following extracts will be found of interest :—" Fingal agreed to hunt in the Forest of Sledale, in company with the Sutherland chief his contemporary, for the purpose of trying the comparative merits of their dogs. Fingal brought his celebrated dog Bran to Sutherland, in order to compete with an equally famous dog belonging to the Sutherland chief, and the only one in the country supposed to be a match for him. The approaching contest between these fine animals created great interest. White-breasted Bran was superior to the whole of Fingal's other dogs, even to the 'surly strength of Luath;' but the Sutherland dog—known by the full-sounding name of Phorp—was incomparably the best and most powerful dog that ever eyed a deer in his master's forests."

Phorp was black in colour, and his points are thus described:—

" ' Two yellow feet such as Bran had,
Two black eyes,
And a white breast,
A back narrow and fair,
As required for hunting,
And two erect ears of a dark red-brown.'

"Towards the close of the day, after some severe runs—which, however, still left the comparative merits of the two dogs a subject of hot dispute—Bran and Phorp were brought front to front to prove their courage; and they were no sooner untied than they sprang at each other and fought desperately. Phorp seemed about to overcome Bran, when his master, the Sutherland chief, unwilling that either of them should be killed, called out—'Let each of us take away his dog.' Fingal objected to this, whereupon the Sutherland chief said with a taunt that it was now evident that the Fingalians did not possess a dog that could match with Phorp.

"Angered and mortified, Fingal immediately extended his 'venomous paw,' as it is called (for the tradition represents him as possessing supernatural power), and with one hand he seized Phorp by the neck, and with the other—which was a charmed and destructive one—he tore out the brave animal's heart. This adventure occurred at a place near the March, between the parishes of Clyne and Wildonan, still called 'Leck na Con' (the stone of the dogs), there having been placed a large stone on the spot where they fought. The ground over which Fingal and the Sutherland chief hunted that day is called 'Dirri-leck-Con.' Bran suffered so severely in the fight that he died in Glen Loth before leaving the forest, and was buried there; a huge cairn was heaped over him, which still remains, and is known by the name of 'Cairn Bran.'"

Our next authority is Bewick (1792). Having described the Irish Wolfhound, he then goes on to say:—"Next to this in size and strength is the Scottish Highland Greyhound or Wolfdog, which was formerly used by the chieftains of that country in their grand hunting parties. One of them, which we saw some years ago, was a large, powerful, fierce-looking dog; its ears were pendulous, and its eyes half hid in the hair; its body was strong and muscular, and covered with harsh, wiry, reddish hair, mixed with white."

The "Encyclopædia Britannica" (1797) says:—"The variety called the Highland Gre-hound, and now become very scarce, is of great size, strong, deep-chested, and covered with long rough hair. This kind was much esteemed in former days, and used in great numbers by the powerful chieftains in their magnificent hunting matches. It had as sagacious nostrils as the Bloodhound, and was as fierce."

There is no allusion to the Deerhound in the "Sportsman's Cabinet," published in 1803; and, curiously enough, but little information regarding him from the beginning of this century up to about 1838, when McNeill wrote regarding him and the Irish Wolfhound in Scrope's book. That the breed *was* kept up in some families will be presently shown— in one case it was claimed that it had been in the owner's family for at least one hundred years. However, be that as it may, we have few, if any, reliable accounts of this dog until McNeill wrote. That gentleman, writing in 1838, says:—"It is not a little remarkable that the species of dog which has been longest in use in this country for the purposes of the chase should be that which is least known to the present generation of naturalists and sportsmen."

Mr. McNeill takes exception to the crosses which had been resorted to by "Glengarry" and others for the purpose of giving increased vigour and size to a breed then rapidly degenerating; but there seems every reason to suppose that had it not been for these judicious crosses the breed would have been almost extinct: at any rate, it would still further have deteriorated. It is very evident, from the following description of Captain McNeill's Buskar, that the Deerhound of forty years ago was a very inferior animal in size and power to the Deerhound of the present day, though possibly he equalled him in courage and speed. Buskar was a sandy-coloured dog, with dark ears, which were nearly erect when excited. He stood 28 inches in height, girthed 32 inches round the chest, and weighed 85 lbs. The hair was hard, not very rough, wiry only on head and legs. He was pupped in 1832, and was looked upon as a remarkably staunch and useful dog. McNeill considered that the purest dogs of his time were sandy or fawn in colour, and hard coated, but he also tells us that "there are dogs in the Lochabar district which are dark in colour and have a softer coat."

From "Chambers's Information for the People," published in 1842, the following extract is taken:—" The Scottish Highland Greyhound will either hunt in packs or singly. He is an animal of great size and strength, and at the same time very swift of foot. In size he equals, if not excels, the Irish Greyhound. His head is long and the nose sharp; his ears short and somewhat pendulous at the tips; his eyes are brilliant and very penetrating, and half-concealed by the long crisp hair which covers his face and whole body. He is remarkable for the depth of his chest, and tapers gradually towards the loins, which are of great strength and very muscular; his back is slightly arched; his hind quarters are powerfully formed, and his limbs strong and straight. The possession of these combined qualities particularly fit him for long endurance in the chase. His usual colour is reddish sand-colour mixed with white; his tail is long and shaggy, which he carries high like the Staghound, although not quite so erect. He is a noble dog, and was used by the Scottish Highland chieftains in their great hunting parties, and is supposed to have descended in regular succession from the dogs of Ossian."

St. John, in his "Wild Sports of the Highlands," published in 1846, says:—" The breed of Deerhounds, which had nearly become extinct, or at any rate was very rare a few years ago, has now become comparatively plentiful in all the Highland districts, owing to the increased extent of the preserved forests and the trouble taken by the different proprietors and renters of mountain shootings, who have collected and bred this noble race of dogs, regardless of expense and difficulties. The prices given for a well-bred and tried dog of this kind are so large that it repays the cost and trouble of rearing him. Fifty guineas is not an unusual price for a first-rate dog, while from twenty to thirty are frequently given for a tolerable one."

"Started this morning at daybreak with Donald and Malcolm Mohr, as he is called (*Anglicé* Malcolm the Great, or Big Malcolm), who had brought his two Deerhounds Bran and Oscar, to show me how they could kill a stag. The dogs were perfect: Bran an immense but beautifully-made dog of a light colour, with black eyes and muzzle, his ears of a dark brown, soft and silky as a lady's hand, the rest of his coat being wiry and harsh, though not exactly rough and shaggy, like his comrade Oscar, who was long-haired and of a darker brindle colour, with sharp long muzzle, but the same soft ears as Bran, which, by-the-bye, is a distinctive mark of high breeding in these days."

The "Museum of Animated Nature," published in 1848—50, has the following:—"In Scotland and Ireland there existed in very ancient times a noble breed of Greyhound, used for the chase of the wolf and the deer, which appears to us to be the pure source of our present breed; it is quite as probable that the Mâtin is a modification of the ancient Greyhound of Europe, represented by the Irish Greyhound or Wolfdog, as that it is the source of that fine breed. Few, we believe, of the old Irish Greyhound exist. In Scotland the old Deerhound may still be met with, and though it exceeds the common Greyhound in size and strength, it is said to be below its ancient standard. With the extirpation of the wolf, the necessity of keeping up the breed to the highest perfection ceased. The hair is wiry, the chest remarkable for volume, and the limbs long and muscular."

Youatt furnishes us with this description of the Deerhound:—"The Highland Greyhound, or Deerhound, is the larger, stronger, and fiercer dog, and may readily be distinguished from the Lowland Scotch Greyhound by its pendulous and generally darker ears, and by the length of hair which almost covers his face. Many accounts have been given of the perfection of its scent, and it is said to have followed a wounded deer during two successive days. He is usually two inches taller than the Scotch Greyhound. The head is carried particularly high, and gives to the animal a noble appearance. The limbs are exceedingly muscular; his back beautifully arched. The tail is long and curved, but assumes the form of almost a straight line when he is much excited. The only fault these dogs have is their occasional ill-temper or ferocity; but this does not extend to the owner and his family."

Richardson, writing about 1848, gives the following regarding the Deerhound:—"The Highland Deerhound presents the general aspect of a Highland Greyhound, especially in all the points on which speed and power depend; but he is built more coarsely and altogether on a larger and more robust scale. The shoulder is also more elevated, the neck thicker, head and muzzle coarser, and the bone more massive. The Deerhound stands from twenty-eight to thirty inches in height at the shoulders; his coat is rough and the hair strong; colour usually iron-grey, sandy, yellow, or white; all colours should have the muzzle and tips of the ears black; a tuft or pencil of dark hair on the tip of the ear is a proof of high blood. This is a very powerful dog, equally staunch and faithful; and when the Scottish mountains swarmed with stags and roes, it was held in high estimation, as being capable of following the deer over surfaces too rough and fatiguing for the ordinary hounds of the low country. The general aspect of the Highland hound is commanding and fierce. His head is long, and muzzle rather sharp; his ears pendulous, but not long; his eyes large, keen, and penetrating, half concealed among the long, stiff, and bristly hair with which his face is covered; his body is very strong and muscular, deep-chested, tapering towards the loins, and his back slightly arched. His hind quarters are furnished with large prominent muscles, and his legs are long, strong-boned, and straight—a combination of qualities which gives him that speed and long endurance for which he is so eminently distinguished. This is the dog formerly used by the Highland chieftains of Scotland in their grand hunting parties, and is in all probability the same noble dog used in the time of Ossian."

The last author treating of the Deerhound that will be alluded to is "Idstone," who brought out his useful book on "The Dog," in the year 1872; but as a considerable portion of the information in the article on the Deerhound therein contained was furnished by the present writer, he will embody it in this treatise as he proceeds. At the same time a few extracts which he cannot lay claim to will not be out of place.

"Until within the last few years the breed was very scarce, for they were kept by the few men who owned the Scotch forests or wide wild tracts of deer-park in the less populated parts of England.

"The fault of the present day with Deerhounds is certainly the short body, the thick, and, as the ignorant consider, the necessarily strong jaw, and the open, loose, flat foot. In proportion to the weight, the foot 'goes,' or deteriorates, and the strain upon a Deerhound's foot at speed amongst stones and boulders, 'in view,' and roused to desperation, is greater than that imposed upon any other domesticated animal. No dog but the 'rough-footed Scot' could stand it.

"The Deerhound is one of the oldest breeds we have. I should be inclined to think that it is an *imported* breed. He is probably identical with the 'Strong Irish Greyhound' mentioned as employed in the Earl of Mar's chase of the red deer, in 1618, by Taylor, in his 'Pennilesse Pilgrimage.'

The oldest strain known is, without doubt, that of the late Mr. Menzies, of Chesthill, on Loch Tay. It is claimed, with every just right, no doubt, that this strain has been in the hands of Mr. Menzies' ancestors for something like eighty to ninety years. Whether it still exists in its integrity the writer is unable to say decidedly; but he is under the impression that as a distinct strain it has disappeared, though there are several dogs in existence that inherit the blood, and that not very distantly. It was asserted that during the time the breed had been in the Menzies family it had only thrice been recruited from outside! Mr. Potter, M.P. for Rochdale, then residing at Pitnacree, Perthshire, had, in 1860, a dog, called Oscar, from Mr. Menzies, and subsequently a bitch, called Lufra, from him. From these many puppies were bred, and given away by him with a liberal hand. A bitch was given to the late Dr. Cox, of Manchester, and from her and Dr. Cox's Ross (by Duke of Devonshire's Roswell, out of Sir R. Peel's Brenda) was bred Buz, the property of Mr. R. Hood Wright, of Birkby Hall, Cark, Carnforth. From this bitch Mr. Wright bred, by a dog (Oscar) of the Duke of Sutherland's breed, his celebrated prize-taker Bevis. It may be here mentioned that Oscar was sold to Prince Albert Solms, of Braunfels, and went to Germany some years ago. The brother to Mr. Cox's Lufra was presented to Menotti Garibaldi, for hunting the mouflon in Sardinia. Oscar, Mr Potter's original Chesthill dog, was given to the late Lord Breadalbane; and descendants of Oscar and Lufra were presented by Mr. Potter to Mr. Cunliffe Brooks, M.P., who, it is believed, has the breed now—indeed, the finest dog at Balmoral lately was one of Mr. C. Brooks's breeding. Mr. Hickman, of Westfield, Selly Hill, near Birmingham, exhibited two brindle dogs at the last Birmingham Show, got by his celebrated Morni out of Garry, by Chesthill Ossian—Lufra. Garry is the property of Mr. Spencer Lucy, of Charlcote. Next to the Chesthill strain, the earliest that the writer knows of is that of Mr. Morrison, of Scalascraig, Glenelg. Mr. John Cameron, of Moy, a farmer residing near Fortwilliam, formerly in service with "Glengarry" as keeper, can remember this breed as far back as 1830. From Bran, a celebrated dog belonging to Mr. Morrison (by him given to McNiel of Colonsay, and afterwards presented by McNiel to Prince Albert), was descended Torrom, the grandsire of Gillespie's celebrated Torrom. The strain of McNiel of Colonsay was known about 1832, and from his strain many of our modern dogs claim descent. The late Mr. Bateson, of Cambusmere in Sutherlandshire, deceased early in 1879, became possessed of a brace of this breed about 1845, named Torrish and Morven. These dogs were sketched by Landseer, the original being now in the hands of Mr. Bateson's family; and he considered them at the time the finest Deerhounds he had ever seen. They were two magnificent dogs, both very rough and of great height and power: Morven reddish in colour, Torrish, darker greyish-brown; Torrish the thickest and biggest in bone, Morven the highest. It is believed this dog left no progeny, though there is an old dog, belonging to the Marquis of Bristol, at Ickworth Park, who is descended in a straight line from his brother Torrish. This dog, Giaour, was bred by Mr. John Bateson, brother to the late Mr. Bateson of Cambusmere, and to him the writer is indebted for all the information regarding these dogs. The breed was entirely in his and his brother's hands from 1845 to the present time, so there can be no doubt regarding its authentic character. The McNiel strain was also owned by Mr. Meredith of Torrish, Sutherlandshire. From a bitch bred by Mr. McNiel, and owned by Mr. Meredith, the Duke of Sutherland's Loyal was bred. Loyal was the dam of the dog Oscar, purchased by Prince Solms, Mr. Cameron's (of Lochiel) Pirate being the sire. As far as can be ascertained, the McNiel dogs in their earliest form were a smaller dog than the present animal, and hardly so rough in the coat, not much exceeding in size the dog, now nearly extinct, that was known as the Scotch Greyhound.

Sir John McNiel was kind enough to furnish the writer, in 1868, with the following information about his breed in later times:—

"The largest and finest dog I ever bred or ever saw was my Oscar. His speed was such that in a straight run he was never beaten by any dog, rough or smooth; and in his best running condition he weighed ninety-four pounds."

From this it will be seen that the McNiel strain had gained both in size and weight since the time Buskar was looked upon as such a wonder.

Another celebrated strain was owned by a Scottish nobleman up to within the last twenty-six years, since which period he has given them up; but some of the blood has passed into other hands, and has been infused in and incorporated with our present strains. The following information furnished by him will be read with much interest:—

"I have never had in my possession a dog above 31 inches. Black Bran, so called to distinguish him from my famous Bran, stood 31 inches in height, and at eighteen months old measured 33½ inches round the chest. He was a first-rate dog. I have seen a dog 34 inches in height, but he was an ill-shaped and utterly useless animal. Sir St. George Gore's Gruim was, I believe, about 32 or 33 inches in height, well-shaped, and a very excellent dog. Gruim was about the year 1843-44, Black Bran about 1850-51, at their best. Bran (the famous) was 29 inches high, and measured 31½ inches round the chest. In shape he was long and low, and so evenly made that he looked much smaller than he really was. He was dark brown at the top of his head—something of the colour of a yell-hind; ears coal black; muzzle black, with a little patch in front of the under-jaw—something like the lips of a roe; back, sides, quarters, and outside of legs yellowish-fawn—deepening in winter time, when his coat was longer, into a sort of yellowish rusty-grey; tail just tipped with white; head quite smooth to behind the ears; ears quite smooth and velvety; coat over body and sides not very long, very harsh and wiry; legs and feet quite smooth; coat, in winter, about three inches long. Bran was at his best about 1844-45. He was entered to his first stag at nine months old (too early), and killed his last stag at nine years old. His greatest feat was the killing of two unwounded stags single-handed in about three-quarters of an hour. The first bore 10 points; the second 11. The pure breed was at one time confined to a very few different kennels. I think my own, and those

DEERHOUND.

of Mr. McNiel, of Colonsay, the late Mr. Stewart Menzies, of Chesthill, and one or two others, were the only gentlemen's kennels in which it was preserved. There were also three or four large farmers in various parts of the country who knew the value of the true breed, and took great pains to preserve the pure strain; but since the great increase of deer forests, in most of which the use of Deerhounds is strictly prohibited, the breeding of these dogs has been very much discontinued, and it is now exceedingly difficult to find one worth anything. Colonel Inge and Lord H. Bentinck have both got my blood. I do not like the Glengarry blood. It was spoilt many years ago by old Glengarry crossing his dogs with the Bloodhound."

The Marquis of Breadalbane, many years ago, owned a famous strain of Deerhounds. They were kept at the Black Mount Forest Lodge. As many as fifty or sixty were kept. A dog called King of the Forest was of extraordinary size. He was an ancestor of a well-known modern prize-taker, also of great size, called Torrom, bred and first exhibited by Mr. Cameron of Lochiel.

The late Sir St. George Gore owned some very fine Deerhounds; one of his is stated to have stood 32 inches. A young dog shown by him, at Birmingham, about thirteen years ago, stood nearly 31 inches, and weighed 105 lbs.; a remarkably fine, well-shaped dog, of a cream colour, but nearly smooth-coated. A bitch, Corrie, brindled, was also large, but poor in coat.

The strain of the late Lord H. Bentinck was very similar to Sir St. G. Gore's—indeed, they bred together for years, and the consequence was that Lord Henry's strain was sadly devoid of coat. A bitch he owned, called Ferret, of McNiel of Colonsay's breed, was smooth, and from her, in all probability, the want of coat was introduced; indeed, in many of the older strains the coat would appear to have been decidedly indifferent, to say the least of it. Lord Henry's Fingal, considered by him to be one of his very best, was a large red dog, almost smooth. From a bitch of this breed, called Carrac, at one time owned by the writer, many of our best modern dogs are descended. At Lord Henry's death his dogs were sold at Edinburgh in 1871, realising by no means large prices.

Some extremely fine Deerhounds were owned many years ago by the late Duke of Leeds.

Mr. Campbell of Monzie, Perthshire, had a very pure breed of Deerhounds about fifteen or twenty years ago. "Lochiel," speaking of them, says:—"I doubt if any Deerhounds except Mr. Campbell's of Monzie are quite pure. There were very few of them left at his death. His was the best and purest blood in the North." From his dog Grumach Mr. Cameron's Pirate and Torrom were bred.

Lieutenant-Colonel Inge of Thorpe for many years bred Deerhounds of remarkably good descent; but he ceased to do so about 1862, when he sent sixteen to be sold at Aldridge's. They fetched prices ranging from 15 to 60 guineas. His celebrated old dog Valiant was bought in at a large figure. They were all well-made dogs and well covered with rough hair, but were not remarkable for size. Colonel Inge had the honour of winning the first prize with Valiant at the first dog show ever held at Birmingham in 1861. He was a very rough brindle dog of lengthy make. Valiant's pedigree was given as by Lord Saltoun's famous Bran out of Seaforth's Vengeance, and he was presented to Colonel Inge when a puppy.

The late Mr. John Cole, for many years head keeper to Her Majesty the Queen at Windsor Park, owned several splendid Deerhounds, bred from Prince Albert's Hector of Monzie's breed, and a bitch of a strain he had brought from Chillingham. At his death the writer purchased three, amongst them the well-known and superb dog Keildar and his sister Hag, a bitch of great size and very good shape, but wanting in coat.

Now to touch on breeders of the present day.

The Duke of Sutherland owns good-looking and useful dogs, but they are small, and a doubt is expressed in some quarters as to their *true* breeding. Regarding some of those *formerly* in his possession there, however, can be no doubt.

Mr. Spencer Lucy of Charlcote has some of the strain of Menzies of Chesthill, as before-mentioned, and has been crossing with one or two well-known prize-takers—it is believed with satisfactory results.

Mr. Gillespie of Tulloch, Kingussie, should be mentioned here, being the breeder and owner of the far-famed Torrom. Though Mr. Gillespie was hardly to be considered a breeder of Deerhounds, yet this dog was such a notoriously good one that, in justice to the subject, notice of his breeder cannot be omitted.

Mr. Donald Cameron of Lochiel is well known to Deerhound lovers as the breeder of Pirate and the giant Torrom. These dogs were from a bitch, Loy, by Mr. Gillespie's Torrom, by Campbell of Monzie's Grumach.

Mr. H. Chaworth Musters is known widely as the owner of the above-mentioned Torrom, which was purchased from "Lochiel" by a Mr. Bowles when exhibited at the Birmingham show in 1869, he then being three years old. He was afterwards purchased by Mr. Musters, and has been extensively bred from, with varied success.

Mr. R. Hood Wright has also bred some very fair Deerhounds. He is mentioned before as having the strain of Menzies of Chesthill in his kennels.

The late Sydney Dobell owned a very capital breed of Deerhound, descended from a bitch presented to him by Flora Macdonald of Skye. These dogs have had much to do with some of the best dogs now extant. They were said to be of pure Glengarry breed.

The last, and perhaps the most successful, breeder to whom allusion will be made is Mr. Thomas Morse. The dogs bred by this gentleman have proved themselves most successful candidates for public favour, and have gone to the top of the tree so far as prize-taking is concerned, and no doubt, where opportunity has offered, have proved themselves as good and true as they unquestionably are good-looking. Amongst them, Mr. Hemming's Linda, Mr. Chinnery's Duke, and Mr. Hay's Rufus, may be mentioned. Mr. Morse decidedly owes much, if not all, of his success to his judicious use of that magnificent dog Keildar, and the produce have in many instances thrown to him in a marked manner, even so far as two generations off.

Before concluding this notice of breeders, the Hon. Mrs. Deane Morgan, living in Co. Wexford, Ireland, should be mentioned, who now has dogs descended from pure strains brought from Scotland many years ago. It is believed these are fine animals, of which their owner is remarkably proud. One was given by her to Mr. George Dennis, Her Majesty's Consul in Sicily, and is reported by him to be an extraordinarily fine and noble animal. Mr. Dennis has lately taken a very well-descended young bitch out to Sicily to mate with him.

Mr. George Cupples has also bred many good dogs, amongst them Spey, now the property of Mr. Morse—selected to illustrate this article. There are several other breeders of years gone by whom the writer had perhaps better mention by name, and though he personally knows but little of their strains, they were reckoned to be remarkably good ones—namely, Lord Seaforth, McDonald of Keppoch, McKenzie of Kintail, and General Ross of Glenmoidart.

It is now proposed to allude to a few of the largest "noted" dogs—before proceeding to describe generally the "cracks" of the breed—that have arisen during the last thirty-five years.

NOTES ON CELEBRATED DEERHOUNDS.

Sir St. George Gore's Gruim has already been noticed. He was said to stand 32 to 33 inches (?), and was a very well-shaped and excellent dog. He was at his prime about 1843-44.

Black Bran, a 31-inch dog, in reality a black brindle, was a remarkably good dog about 1850-51.

The Marquis of Breadalbane's King of the Forest was a dog of extraordinary size, being, it is supposed, 33 inches high. He was held to be a good dog.

An unusually fine dog, called Alder, was shown many times about 1863-67—the property of Mr. Beasley, bred, it was asserted, by Sir John McNiel of Colonsay—that stood about 31½ inches, and probably weighed 110 lbs. This was a very well-shaped dog, not too bulky, of a dark brindle colour; coat very hard. Unfortunately, this dog never got any descendants worthy of himself. He was a grand animal.

In later years we have Torrom, first shown at Birmingham by his breeder, Mr. Donald Cameron of Lochiel, in 1869, he then being three years old. He afterwards passed into the possession of Mr. H. Chaworth Musters, and won numerous prizes, being known as Champion Old Torrom. This dog, as far as could be ascertained, threw back to some ancestor of gigantic size—probably Lord Breadalbane's King of the Forest. He was an extraordinarily heavy dog for a Deerhound, and usually considered lumbersome, and found too much so for work by his owner, who got rid of him for this reason. His head was very massive, and his coat very full and soft; legs by no means straight—a weakness which many of his descendants have inherited. He was a medium brownish colour, faintly brindle, very long in make; ears very coarse, and tail of extreme length. He stood 31 inches, girthed 35, and weighed, *fat*, about 110 lbs.

His two sons — Monzie, out of Brenda, bred by and the property of Mr. Musters, and Young Torrom, out of Braie, bred by Mr. Hancock—are both dogs of great size, standing 31 inches and weighing about 105 lbs.; the former considerably the better dog of the two. The latter dog was exported to America some three years ago.

Of a different strain—going direct back to McNiel's dogs—we have Hector, the property of Mr. Dadley, head-keeper to the Marquis of Bristol—a splendid dog, of darkish brindle colour, good rough coat, and well-shaped, by Giaour, out of Hylda; height, 31 inches; girth, 35; weight, 105 lbs. A good dog with deer, and thoroughly well-bred—probably the best-bred dog now extant.

His two sons—Oscar, the property of Mr. Phillips, Croxton House, Boxford, a very fine symmetrical dog, of great length, rather pale-fawn brindle, out of Lufra, a bitch of small size and somewhat uncertain pedigree, standing 31 inches and weighing about 105 lbs.; and Sir Bors, the property of Lieutenant-Colonel Leyland, a dog of similar colour, out of Lufra also (a prior litter), a very grand dog in every way. He stands 31 inches, girths 35, and weighs 105 lbs.

To go on to a general notice of the cracks. First to be noticed is Mr. Gillespie's celebrated dog Torrom, which is here described in Mr. Gillespie's own words:—"He did not stand very high, but was remarkably well formed for strength and speed; his weight I do not know; colour steel-grey (what we call blue); coat long and silky, with an undergrowth of close downy hair of a darker shade; ears small, and darker in colour than body, with silver-grey dots and tipped with silver-grey silky hair; he also had a great deal of the same silver-grey silky hair on his face; tail long and straight, with half turned to one side when erect; legs very strong, but clean and beautifully formed; feet small, round, and cat-like; chest very deep and round; neck long, arched, and strong; head small, but with wonderful power of jaw (I have seen him break the shoulder of very many red deer stags with a single twist); back very strong and arched; loins of wonderful strength. Torrom was by Faust, a dog (I believe *the last*) that belonged to Mrs. McDonnell, wife of the late Glengarry, and was one of the finest-looking dogs I have seen; his dam was Garry, a bitch given to me by Gordon Cumming when he last started for Africa. On Cumming's return I gave him back the bitch, which I believe he afterwards sold to Sir St. George Gore. Torrom when little more than a year old proved himself the best dog at deer I ever saw or expect to see.

All dogs of any note at the present time can trace their descent back to this exceedingly grand specimen of the race. Mr. Campbell of Monzie's Greumah was a particularly nice dog, got by a fine dog belonging to General Ross of Glenmoidart, of the Keppoch strain, out of a Monzie bitch. He was the sire of Pirate and Torrom, bred by Mr. Cameron of Lochiel. Mr. Cameron writes thus regarding this fine dog:—"He was a magnificent dog, not so massive as his son (Champion Torrom), but more like a Deerhound. He was a strong-framed dog, with plenty of hair, of a blue-brindle colour. He was very like the dog you refer to as belonging to Mr. Gillespie."

Keildar, bred by the late Mr. Cole, head-keeper of Windsor Park, was one of the most elegant and aristocratic-looking Deerhounds ever seen. He was a dog of great length, and yet possessed great speed and power. He was in constant use in Windsor Park for stalking deer, and was very adept at his work. He showed high breeding and symmetry to a remarkable extent. His height was a full 30 inches, girth 33½, and weight 95 lbs.; colour bluish-fawn, slightly brindled, the muzzle and ears being blue; coat rather soft in character and tolerably full. He was by a handsome dog (Oscar), belonging to Mr. Bridge, of the breed of McKenzie of Applecross. His descendants have made their mark by their size, high breeding, and good looks. Amongst them are the well-known Linda, which resembles her sire in an extraordinary degree, his son Rufus, and amongst his grandsons Hector and Duke, Mr. Phillips' Oscar and Lieut.-Colonel Leyland's Sir Bors being his great-grandsons. Mr. Field's Bran, own brother, same litter as Keildar, was only slightly his inferior, and in most ways a very similar dog. Amongst his descendants Morni is perhaps the most remarkable. Mr. Cyril Dobell—brother to Sydney—owned a capital dog of good size in Bevis, the sire of Linda's dam and other good dogs. He was a sandy dog of good coat, stood 30 inches, and weighed probably near 100 lbs., being rather short in make. Major Robertson's Oscar, a nice brindle dog of good coat, long made, bred by General Ross of Glenmoidart, stood about 29 inches, and was a well-made, handsome dog. From him were bred some good dogs out of Sydney Dobell's Maida, and he was the sire of Morni out of a bitch by Field's Bran, out of Carrac.

Mr. Hickman's Morni was a nice dog, of a greyish-brindle colour, coat somewhat soft. He stood 30 inches, girthed 34, and weighed about 98 lbs. Showed quality and breeding.

Pirate, the property of Cameron of Lochiel, and own brother to the celebrated Champion Old Torrom (Mr. Musters'), was a smaller, more compact, and far better-made dog than his gigantic brother. Very dark in colour—blue-brindle—he had a harder and more dense coat than Torrom, and was in every respect his superior. He stood about 29 inches, and was considered "perfect" at work by his owner. He got some very nice stock, but none, it is believed, proved large, though capital dogs for work.

Duke, at one time the property of Mr. Chinnery, winner of several first prizes, was a dark, grizzled, hard-coated dog—perhaps somewhat deficient in hair on head and legs—and a handsome, well-built dog, though somewhat light of bone. He stood 30 inches, and was a fairly lengthy dog.

Spey, the bitch selected for illustration, was bred by Mr. Cupples, and has been owned for many years by Mr. Morse, who has bred many very superior dogs from her. She is about 27 inches in height and of a lengthy frame. Coat very hard and good. Colour is shown in illustration. Duke was her son, and resembled her strongly in coat and colour. She is a well-descended bitch, of thoroughly good appearance.

Mr. Musters' Young Torrom, winner of an extraordinary number of prizes, is a much superior dog to his sire, Old Champion Torrom, but is considerably his inferior in size. He is a dark slate colour, with a lighter head, of not very taking expression, extremely long and strong in make; coat soft and dense. A striking feature in this strain is their very long sweeping tail. His height is about 29½ inches.

Mr. Wright's Bevis, a darkish red-brown brindle dog of about 29 inches, is a thoroughly well-bred dog; perhaps, excepting Hector, the best bred Deerhound out. His coat is very long and shaggy, and extends itself to his ears, very much to the detriment of his appearance. He is a compact, well-shaped dog.

Dr. Haddon has shown a handsome bitch, called Lufra, with a remarkably handsome head and good coat—which former feature she has transmitted to her son, by Young Torrom (Mr. Musters'), Roy by name. The bitch has no ascertained pedigree.

There are many other good and fine dogs scattered through the country which could be mentioned; but as this is not a stud book, it is considered unnecessary to do so.

The Deerhound will now be closely described. As regards size many arguments are put forward. In former days when the red deer was coursed (as hares are) without having previously been wounded, the larger and more powerful the dog was, provided that the Greyhound's speed and activity were preserved, the more was he valued; but in these degenerate days, when deer are usually brought to book without the aid of dogs or often even in their presence, an *animal* that can find and bay a wounded stag is considered to be all that is required. In some few cases the Deerhound proper is used, but this is being fast allowed to fall into disuse in the majority of cases. To run into and hold a full-grown stag, a large and strong dog is certainly required, and it was found that a dog averaging 29 to 30 inches was the correct animal. His girth should be great and chest deep—without being too flat-sided; for a 30-inch dog, 34 inches should be the average. The fore-arm, below elbow, should measure 8½ inches, and the dog weigh from 95 to 105 lbs. Should the dog stand as much as 31 inches, as is sometimes the case, these dimensions would be slightly exceeded. He should be of lengthy make. The average for bitches, which are very much less than the dogs, would be as follows:— Height, 26 inches; girth, 29 inches; weight, 65 to 70 lbs. In figure and conformation this dog should closely approximate to the smooth Greyhound, allowance being made for his superior stature and bulk. The head should be long and lean, rather wider behind the ears, yet not suddenly widening; neck long, strong, and arched; body long; back slightly curved upwards, descending towards tail; legs very strong and straight; feet round, well and firmly set; quarters well-developed, and equal to propelling the animal with extreme velocity; ears small, semi-erect, dark in colour, and smooth, though several strains—really good ones—show a hairy ear; tail long and free from curl, having a curve towards the tip only. The general appearance should be striking, elegant, and aristocratic to a marked extent, and nobility of carriage is a very strong feature in the breed. The coat should be coarse and hard, full and dense on head, body, legs, and tail, without being "exaggerated;" that on the head should be softer in character than that on the body; the hair over eyes and under jaws being of greater length, and rather more wiry than that on the rest of the head. The well-covered head gives much "character," and adds vastly to the general beauty of this magnificent dog. The length of the hair should be from three to four inches. Some breeders hold that no Deerhound is worthy of notice unless he has a good rough head, with plenty of beard and coat generally.; also, that the purity of a smooth skulled dog is to be doubted. Here, however, they are at fault, as several of the best known dogs have had nearly smooth heads.

In colour the Deerhound varies much—from *nearly* black, through dark brindle, blue, light brindle, grey, fawn, and sandy, and cream of all shades, to pure white. Black-and-tan dogs of the breed have also been known. As a matter of taste, the darker colours, as iron-grey and brindle, are to be preferred; but many first-class specimens have been and are of a lighter colour. On a dark heath a light-coloured dog shows plainer.

These dogs are usually remarkably fine and graceful jumpers, and possessed of great activity. In the matter of speed they often equal the smooth Greyhound, but owing to their great size are unequal to making such quick turns as their smaller congener. The scenting powers are developed in a remarkable way, and many wonderful tales are told of the tracking powers of these dogs. When unsighted, they often recover for their masters "cold" stags by their unerring powers in this line.

They are bad swimmers, but occasionally will take the water, and never shrink from it when in pursuit of their quarry.

The Deerhound is justly considered a difficult dog to rear, and to a certain degree delicate, though some authors put him forward as being the "hardiest of the hardy." They also are not a long-lived dog.

It was supposed that the gradual dying out of the practice of coursing the red deer would soon put an end to the breeding of the Deerhound; but such, happily, is not the case. This dog, in reality, has wonderfully increased the last twenty years, and is now, comparatively speaking, common. His beauty, gentleness, power, and courage, have so recommended him as a pet and companion, and his appearance is so ornamental and graceful, that he is highly esteemed by all the gentle in the land; and the fear that the breed would become extinct has long since vanished.

The late Sir St. George Gore, a breeder of experience, was of opinion that the Deerhounds of the present day are far finer than they were thirty and forty years ago; also that a dog could not then be found to run at 85 lbs., whereas now the standard is from 90 to 100 lbs.

Since Lord Henry Bentinck's demise in 1871 no *large* kennels of Deerhounds remain. Formerly there were from twenty to sixty kept in several kennels; at the same time, many magnificent specimens *are* scattered broadcast through the land, as many as six or seven, or even more, being in the same hands, and it is probable that instead of having decreased in numbers it has increased considerably; where *one* person owned a Deerhound or two formerly twenty do so now. Lord Breadalbane, the Duke of Athol, Lord H. Bentinck, "Glengarry," and others, kept large kennels of these superb dogs, but they have all passed away now.

This article will hardly be considered complete unless some allusion be made to the much-vexed question of cross-breeding.

CROSSES USED ON DEERHOUNDS.

"Idstone" says:—" Many crosses have been adopted, as I have already observed, and one of the Deerhound and Mastiff has been used by the proprietor of a deer-pack in my immediate neighbourhood, where there is a fine herd of red and fallow deer. Though I prefer the Deerhound, it must be granted that whilst the breed was not procurable such a measure as manufacturing a dog for the work was meritorious. The best I have noticed of this description were produced by the skill and patience of Mr. Norwood, of the South-Western Railway, at Waterloo. I have never seen these hounds in action, but I have been assured that nothing can be finer than their work. They had the race-horse points, the long neck, the clean head, the bright intellectual eye, the long sloping shoulder, the muscular arms, the straight legs, the close well-knit feet, the wide muscular arched back and loins, the deep back ribs, the large girth, the *esprit*, the life, the activity which when controlled and schooled is essential to every domesticated animal."

It is a well-known fact that the late "Glengarry," finding the breed of Deerhound deteriorating, resorted to several crosses—amongst them the Cuban Bloodhound and Pyrenean Wolfdog; from the latter especially he gained much. He was at the time condemned loudly for thus contaminating the breed; but, in the writer's opinion, he acted with great good judgment, for he resuscitated his strain very completely, and from his so-crossed dogs have all our modern Deerhounds descended, all symptoms of any such cross having long been obliterated. Mr. Gillespie, the owner and breeder of *the* notorious Torrom, says:—"With regard to your remark about the Glengarry dogs not being pure, I too have often heard it; but my *experience* is that there were few, if any, better strains." His Torrom was the son of a true Glengarry dog. Of this breed also was the world-wide-famed Maida, Sir Walter Scott's devoted and constant companion; but he was the offspring of the first cross between Pyrenean Wolfdog and Highland Deerhound, the former being sire, the latter dam. He was a magnificent animal, of great size, power, and endurance, partaking mostly of the appearance of the dam, gaining somewhat in power, bulk, and height from the sire. He was of an iron-grey colour (according to Irving), and of gigantic size. He died at eleven years of age. From this very Maida many of our best modern dogs claim descent!

A gentleman who has had much experience in breeding Deerhounds for the last thirty years and upwards, and who has bred many grand dogs, says:—"My brother informs me that McNiel *went all over the world* to get dogs to breed from—to Albania amongst other places—and that his breed represents a breed he himself founded, and that prior to that there was no real existing breed of Deerhounds in Scotland (! !). I think that their extreme delicacy and the difficulty of rearing them, also the way in which they feel the cold in bad weather in October, indicate their foreign origin."

It is thought that there must have been some misapprehension on this matter, as, putting aside the existence of Morison of Scalascraig's breed in 1830 (McNiel's dating a few years later), as well as that of Menzies of Chesthill, asserted to date from 1780 or thereabouts, Lord Colonsay, then Sir J. McNiel, communicated with the writer about 1865 in the following terms:—" There seems to be no doubt that the Deerhound of the Celtic Highlands is of precisely the same race as the Irish hound sometimes called Wolfhound; and all attempts to get size or speed by crossing have, it is believed, failed, or only succeeded in giving size by destroying the characteristics of the race. I imported Wolfhounds from Russia of fair speed and large size, but silky-haired, with a view to cross them with the Deerhound, but the result was by no means satisfactory. The late Lord Breadalbane crossed with the Bloodhound, and produced some good Retrievers for his deer-stalking; but they were no longer Deerhounds. The Macedonian Dog—a very powerful, smooth dog—was also imported by a member of my family without any better results; and it is my conviction that the race of Deerhounds can be improved only by careful selection and crossing different strains of pure blood."

The above remarks were shown to a friend of the writer who had given a full trial to crossing for size, &c. He says :—"I do not agree with Sir J. McNiel in all he says I think with you that he did not continue his experiments far enough. Then, again, speed was the element he aimed at chiefly, and it is not to be expected he would retain that when crossing with a slower dog."

The writer has not the smallest doubt—looking at the grand dogs we now possess—that the various crosses tried have in most instances profited very much the breed, which had evidently fallen into a degenerate state forty to fifty years ago. He knows by experience that all trace of a cross disappears as a rule in the second or third generation, and the dog has *in every way* the appearance and characteristics of a Deerhound proper. The cross from Russian Wolfhound, judiciously used, has certainly imparted to the Deerhound a degree of quality and certain blood-like look that the breed was fast losing, to say nothing of the gain in the matter of symmetry that almost invariably accrues.

It is a most noticeable and curious fact that the purer the breed is the more marked is the disparity between the sexes in the Deerhound. Thus, if two *pure* bred dogs be used, the difference between the sexes will vary from four to six inches in height; whereas, if the female parent be cross-bred and of large size, the difference between the males and females of the litter will only be two inches, and, oddly enough, even if the bitch so bred shall vastly exceed the truer bred one in size, the dog puppies from her—by an equally fine dog—will generally in no way exceed in size those from the smaller but truer bred bitch.

That size can more surely be obtained through the sire than through the dam is a fact worth remembering.

It is much to be regretted that the pedigrees of the prominent specimens of this breed have not been retained, but there is little doubt but that most of our existing cracks can claim them as their progenitors. In future there will be no trouble on this head, as the very admirable stud-books established about 1870 will obviate this.

Before concluding this article, the writer would strongly impress on all readers the extreme desirability of retaining, by judicious care and cultivation, this, of all dogs (save his undoubted progenitor the Irish Wolfhound), the most beautiful and picturesque, as well as the most majestic and ornamental—an animal to be loved and valued, and treated as a friend, as he richly deserves to be in all but rare cases.

The accompanying engraving, which so faithfully represents some Deerhounds on the watch, is the work of the great German artist, Specht. Though the dogs do not quite come up to modern ideas of show form in every minute particular, the artistic arrangement of the group is to the life, and thoroughly conveys in all essential respects the character of the dog, and what a Deerhound should be.

The dog selected for the coloured plate is Mr. Morse's Spey, who may be taken as one of the best specimens of the breed in existence, though not shown. She was nearly twelve years old in January, 1880, when she scaled 73 lbs., and measured as follows:—From tip of nose to stop, $4\frac{1}{2}$ inches; length from stop to occipital bone, $5\frac{3}{4}$ inches; girth of skull behind the eyes, 15 inches; girth of neck, 15 inches; girth round shoulders, 30 inches; girth of loins, $20\frac{3}{4}$ inches;

SCOTCH DEERHOUNDS.

POINTS OF DEERHOUNDS.

girth of thigh, 16½ inches; girth of forearm, 7 inches; height at shoulders, 26 inches; height at elbows, 14½ inches; height at loins, 26 inches; height at hock, 7½ inches; length of tail, 22 inches. The above must be considered exceptionally good measurements when the advanced age of the dog comes to be considered.

An extremely good bitch, too, which came before the public in 1879, is Heather, the property of the Rev. Grenville F. Hodson, of North Petherton, Bridgwater, which gentleman is one of our oldest Deerhound breeders, and a recognised judge of the variety. Mr. Graham has, we believe, not seen Heather, and has therefore omitted her from the list he gives above.

As in the case of the Irish Wolfhound, Mr. Graham in his article did not append a scale of points. We therefore give the following on our own responsibility.

SCALE OF POINTS FOR JUDGING DEERHOUNDS.

	Value.
Skull	10
Neck	5
Body	10
Legs and feet	10
Coat	10
General appearance	5
Total	50

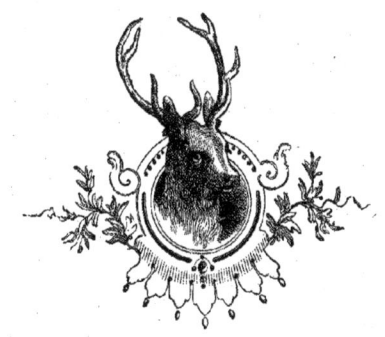

THE SCOTCH DEERHOUND

From his superior size and rough coat the Deerhound has a more imposing appearance than his refined brother the Greyhound, and many would place him at the head of the family. He is frequently referred to as the Staghound. It is well to note this, to prevent confusion, as in England the Staghound is a totally different dog, hunting by scent alone, and often simply a large Foxhound. He is also named the Rough Greyhound, and the Northern, or Fleethound.

Blome, writing of the various hounds of his time, after describing the deep-mouthed hound, says: "For the Northern, or Fleet-hound, his head and nose ought to be slenderer and longer, his back broad, his belly gaunt, his joynts long, and his ears thicker and shorter—in a word, he is in all parts slighter made, and framed after the mould of a Greyhound." It is, however, uncertain whether Blome here meant to describe the Deerhound, or the light-built and swift Foxhound of the North, which, by comparison with the slow, deep-tongued, Southern hound, approached to the Greyhound form.

In that much-valued work the "Sportsman's Cabinet" no mention is made of the Scotch Deerhound, and the Staghound described and illustrated by Reinagle is a pure modern Foxhound.

Richardson, a well-known authority on dogs, writing nearly sixty years ago, gave it as his opinion that the Irish Wolfhound was the ancestor of the Highland Deerhound, an opinion not by any means well supported; this question, however, is discussed at some length in the chapter on the Irish Wolfhound. Equally open to doubt are the crosses suggested by some as having been resorted to in order to prevent the Deerhound from dying out—and particularly those of the Foxhound and Bloodhound.

In treating of the Deerhound, "Stonehenge," who is usually careful and accurate, says: "On carefully examining the description given by Arrian, no one can doubt that the dog of his day was rough in his coat, and in all respects like the present Scotch dog." On the contrary, Arrian is very clear on this point, showing he was well acquainted with both varieties, for he says: "The hair, whether the dog be of the rough or smooth sort," etc. This is quoted in support of the views of a common origin for all the members of this group. "Idstone" is "inclined to think it is an imported breed"; but he gives no reason for thinking so, and declares it "is one of the oldest breeds we have."

Sir Walter Scott did much to draw attention to the breed, and the description of the Deerhound he puts in the mouth of the Knight of Gilsland has never been equalled, and no article on the breed is complete without it: "A most perfect creature of heaven; of the old Northern breed—deep in the chest, strong in the stern, black colour, and brindled on the breast and legs, not spotted with white, but just shaded into grey—strength to pull down a bull, swiftness to cote an antelope."

Of present-day writers none are better qualified to speak than Mr. G. W. Hickman, who has devoted so many years to the practical study of the race as a breeder and judge, and whose literary tastes have naturally led him to make, in addition, a study of its history.

Mr. Hickman's contribution to the last Edition of this work was one of the most interesting and instructive of the many to be found. It combined the historical and the practical in a manner not always, or indeed often, associated. The time that has elapsed since it was published has brought about some slight modifications and changes for the better in the breed as a whole; but Mr. Hickman's advice and words of warning are as sound and necessary now as they were then. We therefore unhesitatingly reproduce as much of the original article as our more restricted space will allow.

"The thing to be feared in connection with the Scottish Deerhound is that the breed, as its use gradually dies out in the Highlands, may lose all its character and quality, and thus be theorised into extinction.

Of late years many men have bred solely for size, and trusted to Providence for quality. The outcome of this has been that we have had on the show-bench animals wanting in all the grace, elegance, and symmetry which should characterise the Deerhound; with big, heavy heads, bulging out at the eyes; with blunt muzzles, nearly as thick at the nose as just in front of the eyes; with big, heavy, drooping ears, often heavily coated and fringed in addition; and with a large but overgrown and weak-looking frame and coarse but doubtful-looking limbs.

I do not say that most of our show dogs have been of this kind, but we have had several notable instances, whose success has been perplexing and disheartening to those who have kept the Deerhound for his proper work, and whose occasional patronage of shows has thus been alienated. This is the more to be regretted, as the use of the Deerhound in his native country is decreasing day by day; and in this fact we come to another of the chief causes which have been prejudicial to the breed, and will be still more so unless care be taken not to lose sight of the purpose for which it was used. As soon as the Deerhound begins to be regarded solely as a show dog, then will the breed be in imminent danger of losing its character; but as long as an animal is bred and used for a practical purpose, so long can reference be made to the product which is found best suited to such requirements.

'Man,' says Darwin, 'closely imitates natural selection'; that is, man in breeding Greyhounds for coursing, Deerhounds for deerstalking, and St. Bernards for use in the snow, selects and breeds from those specimens only which are likely to produce the requisite combination of qualities for his purpose. Thus each product becomes, as far as it can be, a naturally perfect animal for the designed purpose, inasmuch as there is always being applied the infallible criterion of utility and experience to test the results. In each case, mere appearance or outward form has not been the primary consideration with the breeder—the essential qualities are what he aims at; but, finding that those qualities are associated with certain outward characteristics, he is guided by the latter in his selection of breeding specimens. So each breed settles down into a uniform type, and this is maintained by the most rigid of all examiners—experience.

At this point, perhaps, in steps the fancier, or, the man who takes up the breed rather from its appearance than its practical qualities. At first he accepts what he finds, and does not get far away from the proper type; but presently, as he has no other means of testing his results, he lays down certain rules or points for his guidance, and very often attaches undue importance to some one of these that readily strikes the eye, forcing it unduly to the expense of, and out of its proper relation to, the rest; and as he does not apply the touchstone of a practical trial in its proper vocation to his production, he errs more and more in the direction of his arbitrary requirements, and the breed loses that harmony of combined qualities which constituted its original 'character,' and which had been kept in due relation by practical requirements.

That the Deerhound has suffered considerably from a mania for size is only too certain, and that it will suffer more yet is to be feared, unless judges will set their faces against allowing themselves to be influenced by mere size and bulk. In proof of my assertion, subjoined is an extract from a letter received, some quarter of a century ago, from a gentleman who bred and exhibited some of the best specimens when shows were in their infancy:

'Some twenty years ago, before shows began, there were two or three owners of the breed, and a few dogs might be called pure.

The late Duke of Leeds had as pure blood of the old breed as any one. After shows were the fashion, great size, at the expense of other qualities, was considered necessary, and lately there has been much resort to crossing. I am an advocate for size myself, but speed must not be sacrificed to it. If you desire a true guide to tell whether a dog has been crossed, look at his ear first. If that is SMALL, and lies folded close to his head, like a Greyhound's, I should consider *that* a very great point in his favour as to his purity; but if his ears droop, and are large, no matter what his size and appearance were, I should be quite certain he had a cross somewhere. I consider size and shape before colour, and the purest dogs of old time had little white upon them—the less the better on the feet and legs; but colour is always a superficial matter, and can always be regulated as the breeder chooses. Size and FORM, especially combining strength and great speed, are far more difficult to obtain.'

I can commend every word of the foregoing to the careful consideration of every admirer of the Deerhound, especially those with regard to the ear, as close observation has convinced me of their perfect truth, as I have invariably noticed, in those strains which have been notoriously crossed within a recent period, that, though they might pass muster in other respects, they had large, heavy, hanging ears.

As regards the size required in the Deerhound for work in the Highlands, there seems to be no doubt that a dog over 30in. at the shoulder would be useless. Indeed, one authority, whose family claim to have kept the purest breed in the Highlands, solely for work, for upwards of the last sixty years, puts the height at 26in. up to 28in. He says: 'Larger dogs may be good enough for racing, but for hard work, so far as my experience has gone, I always found an ordinary sized dog do his work much better.'

The following opinions of the two greatest authorities that could be produced, Lochiel and Horatio Ross, Esq., must convince even those who, by their arguments and aims, seem to think that the Deerhound can never be too large for his work. The former observes: 'Personally, I do not like dogs over 30in., and prefer them between 28in. and 30in. They get too coarse at a great height, and quite useless for real work. Great size too often depends on feeding, and if thus produced gives a coarse and soft dog, quite unsuited for the purpose for which he is intended.' The latter states, that for deerstalking a height of '28in. to 30in. is ample. A very large dog is never a good dog; he gets beat going up hill.' What is the use of theory against opinions like these?

The late Lieut.-Colonel Inge, who for many years possessed one of the most extensive deer forests in Scotland, and whose kennel of

Deerhounds fetched large prices on their disposal at Aldridge's many years ago, was of the same opinion, and informed my father that large dogs were useless for deerstalking. I have had personal knowledge of five kennels of Deerhounds, kept for work alone in the Highlands, and from all connected with them I have always heard the same opinion expressed as to the uselessness of the very large dogs. In the case of three noted show dogs of late years, all about 31in. high, and of another that created a sensation in America, I was informed by each of their owners that they were parted with because they were too big for work in the Highlands—and not one exceeded 31in. at the shoulder, and three of them were symmetrical, and well made for big dogs. These three were (Old) Torunn, Bran (1st prize, Crystal Palace, 1872), and Sir Boriss. The remaining one was never exhibited in England. It will be recollected, perhaps, that McNeil's Buskar, the largest of the dogs which took part in the deer course described in the Appendix to Scrope's 'Deerstalking,' was only 28in. in height. Those who wish to see the original of Landseer's sketch will find it in the Bell Collection in the National Gallery. The animal certainly looks rather light in substance, but it is fair to call to mind that McNeil, referring to it, stated that the portrait scarcely gave a correct idea of the muscle and bone of the original; and this must have been so, as the dog girthed 32in., or 4in. more than its height, and few Deerhounds exceed, or attain to, this proportionate depth of chest. McNeil's dogs, as is well known, were used for coursing the deer in the Island of Jura, and from the very fact of the place being an island, the practice was not subject to the disadvantages which it would have been on the mainland, by driving the deer far away. Now, if McNeil's dogs, which did not exceed 28in. in height, were equal to the task of coursing and pulling down a cold (*i.e.* unwounded) stag, it seems reasonable to infer that a larger dog could hardly be necessary for deerstalking where it was only, or chiefly, used for the purpose of retrieving the wounded deer.

From the above remarks and authorities it will be gathered that very large dogs are of little use in deerstalking. It must not, however, be supposed that I would necessarily confine the show Deerhound within the same limits. Everyone likes a fine, upstanding dog, and a little extra height may, perhaps, be tolerated in a show dog; but what is deprecated is the awarding of a prize to a dog simply and solely because he is large, coarse, and bulky—in fact, for the very and only reason that he possesses those qualities which would entirely unfit him for the purpose which his names implies. Personally, I think dogs of 30in. tall enough for anything; and that, instead of trying to raise them beyond this, the efforts of breeders would be more usefully directed to improving their quality, and obtaining the requisite combination of strength and speed.

The causes of the disuse of the Deerhound in the Highlands are, as is pretty well known, the greater precision of modern rifles, and the great demand for, and consequent sub-division of, deer forests and shootings. Years ago, when the large Highland proprietors, or chieftains, held their vast tracks in their own possession, before they had begun to realise what a gold mine their barren hills and wild expanse of heather contained, it mattered little how much the deer were disturbed or how far they were driven. But now that forests, by sub-division, have become far more numerous, and as nothing frightens away deer more than chasing them with Deerhounds, the use of the latter has died away, and, indeed, is prohibited in many leases.

Another circumstance which threatens to seriously injure and coarsen the Deerhound is the modern craze that seeks to identify the Irish Wolfhound, long extinct, with a gigantic Deerhound. To attain the required standard, the Deerhound has been crossed with various large breeds, even, I believe, with the St. Bernard; but the results have not been satisfactory, as, though bulk and coarseness have been obtained, the height does not appear to have been increased. Some of the animals thus bred have found their way on to the show-bench as Deerhounds, and will certainly, with their mixed blood, do no good to the breed if they transmit the qualities for which themselves are conspicuous.

Having now seen what the Deerhound, in my opinion, was not, let us see what he is. He is doubtless the tall, rough Greyhound of ancient days, appointed, as Holinshed says, to hunt the larger beasts, such as stags and the like, and probably at one time as common in England as in Scotland. The disappearance of the larger animals in a wild state from England at such an early period contrasted with Scotland would account for his being found in the latter country so long a time after he had totally died away here. There can, indeed, be no doubt, from the accounts of Caius and Holinshed, and those we get from others, that large 'shagg-haired' Greyhounds were used in England. This affords another inference against the theory of Richardson, for, if the Irish dog had been no more than a large, rough Greyhound, it would not have been in any way remarkable. It was clearly a specific animal, peculiar to Ireland, which merely rough Greyhounds evidently were not. The Russian Wolfhound is an analogous example of the tall, rough Greyhound of ancient days, yet I have never heard it claimed as an Irish Wolfdog.

Captain Graham, in 'The Book of the Dog,' says the earliest record of the Deerhound is that given by Pennant, in 1769, and elsewhere he founds thereon one of the chief inferences for his Wolfdog theory, 'that, whilst we have accounts of all the noticeable breeds from a remote period, including the Irish Wolfdog, we do not find any allusion to the Deerhound, save in writings of a comparatively modern date, which in a measure justify us in supposing that the Deerhound is the modern representative of that superb animal.' Now, if my theory is correct that the Deerhound is simply the tall, rough Greyhound used for hunting the larger game, this apparent want of allusion is explained, as we have plenty of references to such Greyhounds. It is remarkable that, to this day, the Deerhound is often called 'a Greyhound' by the Highlanders. A gentleman informed me, some years ago, that his forester always used the term 'Greyhound,' and I have letters from gentlemen in the Highlands in which the terms Greyhound, Staghound, and Deerhound are used indifferently; in fact, Deerhound is a term even now far less in use than Staghound.

We cannot, therefore, feel surprised if we do not meet the term 'Deerhound' in old times, when we get mention of the Greyhound under the term of Highland Greyhound, or its equivalent. The 'Irish Greyhounds' mentioned by Taylor, in 1620, were most certainly Deerhounds; but, to save any quibbling on terms, I will now proceed to show that the specific word 'Deerhound' was used long ago, before any degeneracy from the Wolfdog can be supposed. In Pitscottie's 'History of Scotland,' published about 1600, occurs the following passage: 'The king (A.D. 1528) desired all gentlemen that had dogges that war guid to bring thame to hunt in the saidis boundis, quhilk the most pairt of the noblemen of the Highlandis did, sick as the Earles of Huntlie, Argyle, and Athol, who brought their deir houndis with thame and hunted with his majestie.'

This authority is decisive, and completely shatters the last possible remnant of the chief argument for the identification of the Irish Wolfdog with the Deerhound. The inference that both were the same is met by the irresistible fact that the Irish dog was imported into Scotland when the Deerhound existed in large numbers, and at a period when it cannot have degenerated. The further inference of the Richardsonians, that with a change of occupation came a change of name, and that the name Deerhound was not used until very late times, when the Wolfdog had degenerated into the Deerhound, is shown to be utterly unfounded by the fact of the use of the name Deerhound three hundred years ago. The last pretence for such an inference is now destroyed.

In modern times the breed of Mr. Menzies, of Chesthill, is doubtless the oldest strain we have note of. A gentleman who knows the district well, and purchased a dog called Ossian at Menzies of Chesthill's sale some years ago, informed the writer that the family claimed to have had the breed pure for one hundred years. Ossian is the grandsire of my Champion Cuchullin.

Next in point of antiquity would come the strain of Mr. Grant, of Glenmoriston, for Captain Basil Hall, who described his dogs in 1848, and who therefore saw them, probably, a year or so before, mentions that Mr. Grant had kept the breed thirty years, which would take us back to about 1815 or so. I have never seen Captain Basil Hall referred to in relation to the Deerhound, though his account is highly interesting. He states that the first dog Glenmoriston had was sent him by Captain Macdonald, of Moray in the Braes of Lochaber. Having heard of a pure and beautiful bitch, celebrated for her great courage and lasting power, then the property of Mr. Mackenzie, of Applecross, Glenmoriston suggested to him that one of them should keep up the breed. Mr. Mackenzie declined, and the bitch became domiciled at Invermoriston, from which period—then about forty years ago—the breed had remained uncontaminated in those parts. Captain Hall then remarks that he had since learnt that Glenmoriston had relinquished the breed to Mr. E. Ellis, of Glengarry.

The breed of McNeil of Colonsay, described in Scrope's work in 1839, would be the next one of which we have any account. His dogs have been already described.

It may here be mentioned that Captain Hall states that he had two Glenmoriston dogs, and one from another source, and that he gave one to a friend in Ireland. It was, perhaps, some of the descendants of this latter dog that Captain Graham's friend mistook for Wolfdogs in the early part of the 'Forties' of this century. At all events, we see that Deerhounds had been sent to Ireland.

General Hugh Ross and Colonel David Ross had also a fine kennel in Glenmoidart some years ago, the remains of which, including Oscar, winner of first prize Birmingham in 1865 and 1866, passed into the hands of their relative Major Robertson, who, unfortunately, lost the stud records. I have no very distinct recollection of Oscar, but he has been described to me by the breeder of Morni—whose sire Oscar was—as a dog not over large, but with grand hindquarters and thorough Deerhound character. Colonel Campbell, of Monzie, was also noted for his kennel of Deerhounds some thirty years or more ago. I never saw but one actually bred by Monzie—an elegant yellow dog, called Rob, exhibited by Mrs. Cameron Campbell, at Birmingham, in 1870, good sized, and with plenty of character. Monzie's Gruamach, the sire of Lochiel's Torunn (afterwards belonging to Mr. Musters) and Pirate, is perhaps the best known of this strain. He was, doubtless, a very fine dog, and I may perhaps be permitted to mention, without being charged with egotism, that I was informed by a gentleman who has kept Deerhounds for work for nearly thirty years, and who was well acquainted with Monzie's dogs, and bred from them, that Gruamach and Morni were the two finest Deerhounds he had ever seen. The same gentleman informed me—*horresco referens*—that Gruamach, in his old age, was killed and eaten by his kennel companions! This is the worst blot on the Deerhound's character that I ever knew, and is almost incredible. In conversation, some years after, with the kennelman who had charge of the dogs at the time, he repeated the circumstance, with particulars. It appears that Gruamach had been the master of the kennel so long, that his younger companions rose one night in a body against his tyranny, and treated him as I have described.

Perhaps the happiest hit ever known in breeding show Deerhounds was made by my friend Mr. Pershouse Parkes when he sent Brenda, the own sister to Morni, to Mr. Musters's Torunn. The one litter contained such noted dogs as Mr. Musters's Torunn (the Younger), Mr. H. P. Parkes's champion bitch Teeldar, Lord St. Leonard's Hylda, and Mr. Lewis's Meg, all great winners on the show-bench at Birmingham and the other large shows. In addition to this, their blood, or that of their near relative Morni, is to be found in nearly every show dog of the present day.

As an example of the uncertainty in choosing a puppy in dogs like the Deerhound, it may be mentioned that Morni and his sister Brenda were the two selected by their breeder for weeding out from a litter of six. I selected the dog for a small sum, and the bitch was given away to a friend. The one grew up into Champion Morni, the most successful show dog of his day, though he retired at six years old; and the other became the dam and ancestress of more prize winners than any other bitch that can be mentioned. Such is luck. Allowance must be made for the fond prejudice of ownership, and perhaps a discount taken off accordingly; but I cannot call to mind a dog that combined in a greater degree than Morni the qualities of symmetry and strength: of a good height, and a greater proportionate length than is usually seen, he nevertheless possessed an extremely deep chest and enormous loin, with a wonderful breadth of hindquarters, a grand forearm, and yet withal a perfect Greyhound frame. There was, moreover, that appearance of quality and character which is so wanting in some specimens nowadays. One fault was ever found with him—viz. that his coat was too soft; but that arose from the way he was treated, in being made a pet of. Had he been kept out in a kennel, and roughed it, the coat would have been hard enough; and, as it was, it was hardness itself to that of most of the prize winners we have seen since. Morni had but few chances given him at the stud, his services being only allowed to a select few. He was chiefly used by a gentleman who bred dogs for work alone, and the few of his progeny that have found their way on to the show-bench have been odd dogs out of such litters. Nevertheless, every dog but one by him that has been shown has been a prize winner; and, what is more, the pups that were bred for work all showed themselves possessed of speed, courage, and all the qualities of the Deerhound in their vocation in the Highlands.

Lochiel's Pirate was one of the finest dogs I ever saw; he stood about 29in., had good bone, fine symmetry, and a hardish coat of a fair length, and altogether looked what a Deerhound should—a combination of speed and power. He was of the dark blue colour, so much prized, and so seldom seen. The Duke of Sutherland exhibited two very fine dogs of this colour at Birmingham in 1869, and a descendant of theirs, in the person of Lord Fitzhardinge's Tom, a powerful dog of like colour, took first at Birmingham in 1880. Another beautiful dog, in shape and symmetry, was Mr. J. Addie's Arran, a well-known dog some thirty years ago. He stood over 30in. at the shoulder, had a wonderfully deep chest, capital loin, strong limbs of the best shape, and was of a dark blue colour, approaching black. His great failing was his want of coat, it being extremely scanty, especially on the head and legs. From the union with Mr. Parkes's Brenda he is the grandsire of that gentleman's Borva and Leona and of my Lord of the Isles, in all of which dogs some of his best qualities can be traced. Wallace, son of Arran, was a well-shaped dog, of but medium height, perhaps not more than 28in. For this reason, and from a deficiency of coat as a puppy, he was not destined to the show-bench, but given away. He afterwards, I am told, developed a splendid coat; but it was almost by a chance that Mr. H. P. Parkes bred from him, as he was thought not to have sufficient size. The result was, however, that his first litter produced some dogs of the largest size in Lord of the Isles, Mr. Parkes's Duncan, and Mr. Sherman's Haco. Duncan, whose loss Mr. Parkes never ceased to regret, though larger than I care for, was certainly the best-made giant I can call to mind. His owner states that he was $31\frac{1}{2}$in. in height, girthed 35in., and weighed 97lb., at thirteen months old, when he was exhibited for the first time. He then caught distemper and died, as so many puppies do. Haco was over 29in. high at nine months old, when purchased by me for Mr. W. S. Sherman, of Rhode Island, and sent out to America. On his voyage out he was shipwrecked on his 'native' shore of Scotland, off the Mull of Cantyre; but after being transhipped he arrived safely at his destination, and won first prize at the great New York Show in 1881.

Wallace's second litter from the same bitch produced Mr. Parkes's Borva and his well-known bitch Leona, the latter one of the best of her time. Borva was a true Deerhound, a wonderfully fast dog and a magnificent fencer, and would have made a perfect dog for work. Owing, however, to his not being an overgrown animal, but only about 28in., he was not so successful as a show dog as he should have been.

Here we have the case of a moderate-sized dog like Wallace

getting unusually large stock ; showing that, if an animal has size in its breeding, it is just as likely to transmit size as one of its larger relations, thus giving encouragement to the plan, advocated by me, of not always selecting the largest and coarsest specimens of a strain in the hope of getting size merely because they are big, a system which simply perpetuates coarseness and clumsiness, very often unaccompanied by what is the chief aim. But if you breed from the smaller specimens of a large strain which possess character and quality, you will be nearly sure to get the latter, and very probably the size : 'a giant's dwarf may beget a giant.' Dr. Hemming's Linda, whose portrait was given in the First Edition of this work, was a splendid bitch, but her portrait was a mere caricature, and must have been taken in the last stage of decrepitude and decay.

It has been a matter of remark how much superior in late years the bitches have been to the dogs. For one good dog we can count three or four good bitches. Amongst the latter Dr. Haddon's Maida must not be forgotten. She was a grand bitch, with a fine coat, and would doubtless have been the greatest prize winner of her sex, had she not been killed in transit to the Alexandra Palace Show before she had got to her best. Mr. Parkes's Teeldar and Leona were also of the highest class, and several others I might mention. Indeed, a long string of first-class ones could be given, beside which an equal number of the dogs contemporary with them would make a poor show.

The great fault of the show Deerhound of to-day is the want of length and Greyhound form, the coarse, thick muzzles, heavy ears, woolly coats, and want of quality, arising from breeding for size alone. A dog standing 30in. at the shoulder, girthing 33in. to 34in., and with a loin of not less than 24in. round, should be the highest standard aimed at. The rest of our efforts should be directed to getting the highest combination of strength and speed with the greatest amount of character, aiming at improving the length to such a degree that the dog should, with all his size, have a long, low frame, rather than a tall, stilty one.

As companionable animals, Deerhounds cannot be excelled. Their chief drawback is their eagerness, when young, to chase any running object. If, however, they are taken out constantly, or reared amongst animals in the country, they soon become easily restrainable and capital followers. They are not quarrelsome, but when they get three or four years old will not stand any nonsense from other dogs. They are of a gentle and affectionate disposition, strong in personal attachment, and may safely be let run about the premises without any fear of their biting any lawful comer. They are delicate dogs to rear, and should never be shown as puppies unless they have had distemper.

The great difference in size between dogs and bitches of this breed has often been a matter of notice ; and, as has been often correctly remarked, the purer the breed the greater the difference. Crossing increases the height of bitches, but not so much so that of the dogs. I do not believe in crossing; but, if it be resorted to, the best cross, there can be no question, is that with the Russian Wolfhound, a very pure bred dog, and of an analogous breed. Improvement in Greyhound shape might certainly be looked for, and the chief defects to be expected are the soft, silky coat and

FIG. 37.—MR. R. HOOD WRIGHT'S SCOTCH DEERHOUND SELWOOD DHOURAN.

the white colour. But plenty of material is at hand nowadays, if breeders will have the courage not to neglect good strains simply because they are not of very large size."

It must not be imagined that the breeders enumerated by any means exhaust the list of those who are entitled to rank as among the more noteworthy even. No article upon the Scotch Deerhound would be complete that did not give credit to the brothers Bell, of Forgandenny, for the many fine hounds produced within their kennels; or to the indefatigable Mr. Hood Wright, who has laboured so long for the breed whose cause he has chiefly espoused, and who, moreover, has shown all those practical qualities that go to make a successful fancier. Like the Bells, his name has been associated with a host of good dogs, of which Selwood Morven, that afterwards passed into the hands of Mr. Harry Rawson, Selwood Dhouran, and Selwood Boy are but a trio that come readily to mind. Mr. W. H. Singer, too, at one time owned and bred some noteworthy specimens, of which Champion Swift was the best known. Of other names writ large on the scroll of Deerhound fame, those of the Duchess of Wellington, Mr. W. Evans, Mr. G. E. Crisp, Mr. Morse Goulter, Mr. W. B. Gibbin, Mr. W. C. Grew, Major Davis, Dr. and Miss Rattray may be named. Fig. 37 illustrates Champion Selwood Dhouran, a dog that has had a most remarkable show-ring career. He stands over 31in. at shoulder, and is by Champion Swift (30,617) out of Selwood Morag (37,981).

Mr. Hickman has already referred to the good qualities of the Deerhound as a companion, and he certainly does not at all colour the picture. Of recent years the Kennel Press has received many testimonials from ladies testifying to the full to the hounds' excellent qualities. What has been said in respect of the Irish Wolfhound as regards details of management, colour of puppies, etc., apply equally to the Scotch hound, which only needs to be better known to be more highly appreciated.

The following excellent description of the Scotch Deerhound was drawn up by Mr. Hickman and Mr. Hood Wright, and it received the approval of the Scottish Deerhound Club in 1892:—

Head.—The head should be broadest at the ears, tapering slightly to the eyes, with the muzzle tapering more decidedly to the nose. The muzzle should be pointed, but the teeth and lips level. The head should be long, the skull flat, rather than round, with a very slight rise over the eyes, but with nothing approaching a stop. The skull should be coated with moderately long hair, which is softer than the rest of the coat. The nose should be black (though in some blue-fawns the colour is blue), and slightly aquiline. In the lighter-coloured dogs a black muzzle is preferred. There should be a good moustache of rather silky hair, and a fair beard.

Ears.—The ears should be set on high, and, in repose, folded back like the Greyhound's, though raised above the head in excitement without losing the fold, and even, in some cases, semi-erect. A prick ear is bad. A big thick ear, hanging flat to the head, or heavily coated with long hair, is the worst of faults. The ear should be soft, glossy, and like a mouse's coat to the touch, and the smaller it is, the better. It should have no long coat or long fringe, but there is often a silky, silvery coat on the body of the ear and the tip. Whatever the general colour, the ears should be black or dark-coloured.

Neck and Shoulders.—The neck should be long—that is, of the length that befits the Greyhound character of the dog. An over-long neck is not necessary, nor desirable, for the dog is not required to stoop to his work like a Greyhound, and it must be remembered that the mane, which every good specimen should have, detracts from the apparent length of neck. Moreover, a Deerhound requires a very strong neck to hold a stag. The nape of the neck should be very prominent where the head is set on, and the throat should be clean-cut at the angle and prominent. The shoulders should be well sloped, the blades well back and not too much width between them. Loaded and straight shoulders are very bad faults.

Stern.—Stern should be tolerably long, tapering, and reaching to within 1½in. of the ground, and about 1½in. below the hocks. When the dog is still, dropped perfectly straight down, or curved. When in motion it should be curved when excited, in no case to be lifted out of the line of the back. It should be well covered with hair, on the inside thick and wiry, underside longer, and towards the end a slight fringe not objectionable. A curl or ring tail very undesirable.

Eyes.—The eyes should be dark, generally they are dark brown or hazel. A very light eye is not liked. The eye is moderately full, with a soft look in repose, but a keen, far-away look when the dog is roused. The rims of the eyelids should be black.

Body.—The body and general formation is that of a Greyhound of larger size and bone. Chest deep rather than broad, but not too narrow and flat-sided. The loin well arched and drooping to the tail. A straight back is not desirable, this formation being unsuitable for going up-hill, and very unsightly.

Legs and Feet.—The legs should be broad and flat, a good broad fore arm and elbow being desirable. Fore legs, of course, as straight as possible. Feet close and compact, with well-arched toes. The hindquarters drooping, and as broad and powerful as possible, the hips being set wide apart. The hind legs should be well bent at the stifle, with great length from the hip to the hock, which should be broad and flat. Cow hocks, weak pasterns, straight stifles, and splay feet very bad faults.

Coat.—The hair on the body, neck, and quarters should be harsh and wiry, and about 3in. or 4in. long; that on the head, breast, and belly is much softer. There should be a slight hairy fringe on the inside of the fore and hind legs, but nothing approaching "the feather" of a Collie. The Deerhound should be a shaggy dog, but not overcoated. A woolly coat is bad. Some good strains have a slight mixture of silky coat with the hard, which is preferable to a woolly coat, but the proper coat is a thick, close-lying, ragged coat, harsh or crisp to the touch.

Colour.—Colour is much a matter of fancy. But there is no manner of doubt that the dark blue-grey is the most preferred. Next come the darker and lighter greys or brindles, the darkest being generally preferred. Yellow and sandy-red or red-fawn, especially with black points—*i.e.* ears and muzzles—are also in equal estimation, this being the colour of the oldest known strains, the McNeil and the Chesthill Menzies. White is condemned by all the old authorities, but a white chest and white toes, occurring as they do in a great many of the darkest-coloured dogs, are not so greatly objected to, but the less the better, as the Deerhound is a self-coloured dog. A white blaze on the head or a white collar should entirely disqualify. In other cases, though passable, yet an attempt should be made to get rid of white markings. The less white the better, but a slight white tip to the stern occurs in the best strains.

Height of Dogs.—From 28in. to 30in., or even more if there be symmetry without coarseness, but which is rare.

Height of Bitches.—From 26in. upwards. There can be no objection to a bitch being large, unless too coarse, as even at her greatest height she does not approach that of the dog, and, therefore, could not have been too big for work, as over-big dogs are. Besides, a big bitch is good for breeding and keeping up the size.

Weight.—From 85lb. to 105lb. in dogs; from 65lb. to 80lb. in bitches.

BREEDING, PUPPING, AND REARING.

"IT is surprising how soon a want of care, or care wrongly directed, leads to the degeneracy of a domestic race." Thus speaks Mr. Darwin in his "Descent of Man," and no practical breeder of any sort of stock can be found to disagree with him. No care and attention on the part of the owner and his servants can turn a badly-bred, ill-formed animal into a good one; and though it is impossible to bestow too much consideration on the treatment of the stock, all exertions on behalf of animals badly bred will be, as a rule, thrown away when they come before the judge. Years of anxiety go for nothing, if due attention is not paid not only to the health and strength, but also to the proper selection of the breeding stock. As in the articles on the various breeds full prominence has been given to the special points which must be studied in each individual variety, it is unnecessary here for us to go beyond a general outline of the management of what may be called the breeding materials.

It is wonderful to reflect upon the success which seems to attend the efforts of some of the most loosely-conducted establishments, and to see winner after winner turned out from a kennel where no rules of breeding are for a moment studied, and where the management is often left by the owner in the hands of a kennel-man whose knowledge of the breed is absolutely *nil*. Such success in the few instances in which it occurs is eventually unfortunate in its results, both to the breeders of the dogs themselves and also to many of the outside world, who, either to save themselves trouble, or through ignorance of the simplest principles of breeding, ignorantly rush for the services of the nearest prize-winner, utterly regardless as to whether he is likely to "nick" with the bitch they propose uniting with him, in shape, size, or pedigree. The result may be a temporary success, but is certain ultimate destruction of all type. Breeding *can* be regulated by rules and judicious selection, else how do we see so many breeds of dogs now in existence (which we can prove to have originated from a cross of two older varieties) keep on throwing puppies which consistently resemble their parents in every property, and whose difference from them only consists in minor insignificant and immaterial features? By rigidly adhering to an ideal type, and resisting all temptations to go from it, a breeder is certain in time to find himself in possession of the sort of dog he has, rightly or wrongly, determined on possessing; and then he is in a position to discover, from the success of his dogs, whether his exertions are to be repaid or not.

We must commence, then, by impressing upon all beginners, and many older hands, the desirability of adhering to *one type* if they want to make a name for themselves as amateur breeders. Of course, in the case of those who breed solely for the market it is right that they should produce good specimens of every recognised standard, so as to please buyers, whatever their own opinions may be; but as these remarks are not intended to be addressed to dealers, who are perfectly competent to manage their own business, but to amateurs, it is sufficient to point out the importance of adhering to one type. By breeding to one standard, we necessarily imply that no one should be induced to set up as a producer of canine stock until he has clearly made up his mind what sort of animal he wishes for. In the case of a beginner, there is generally an acquaintance at hand who possesses more or less experience in such matters, and who, if he be a real lover of the dog, will be glad to place his services at his young friend's disposal. The opinions of such an individual may not all be correct; but if he be fairly competent, and honest, he can always be useful to the beginner. It is a great assistance, too, in arriving at a correct opinion, if the uses for which the various breeds have been brought into existence are brought under consideration. It is no good breeding a dog, though he be ever so handsome-looking, if he is palpably unfit for the work he is supposed to perform if called upon; and, under a judge who knows his work, a flashy-looking dog often has to lower his colours to his more sober and workman-like neighbour, whose undoubted good properties have escaped the attention of the uninitiated.

Having decided upon the type which he himself desires to produce, a beginner should make it his next business to ascertain if his ideas in any way resemble the orthodox standard; if so, his labours are considerably diminished, as his object in breeding will be to obtain the services of such stud dogs as he particularly admires, and in whose pedigree he has satisfied himself there is no bar sinister. It is an indisputable fact that a well-bred dog is far more likely to beget stock resembling himself than a good-looking mongrel is. Again, in the case of the former, even if he fails to impress his own likeness on his progeny, there is a possibility, if not a fair amount of certainty, that the puppies will throw back to a well-bred ancestor of more or less elegant proportions; whilst with a dog whose pedigree is enveloped in mystery or something worse, there is a chance of the young ones displaying every conceivable type and temper.

The subject of in-breeding is one which has exercised the minds of breeders for many a day, and affords matter for a controversy which seems far from being brought to a termination. There can be no sort of doubt that, if carried to too great a length, in-breeding stunts the growth and weakens the intelligence and constitution of all dogs. This opinion is, we believe, unanimously received by all breeders of canine stock; though, in the case of game-cocks more than one authority has it that incestuously-bred birds are stouter, gamer, and more active than those whose parents are unrelated to each other. Observation has proved that the union of father with daughter and mother with son is far preferable, where dogs are concerned, to an alliance between brother and sister. Once in and twice out is, we believe, an excellent system if the crosses are judiciously selected, and the reasons for this appear to be as follows:— A breeder has a dog belonging to a strain which usually produces good-headed ones, but apt to be leggy and perhaps deficient in coat. He naturally wishes to remedy these defects, and in many instances selects as a mate a dog indifferent in head, but good in bone and in jacket; the result being most probably one fair puppy and several very indifferent ones which inherit the faults of both their sire and dam. On the other hand, however, had he exercised a little patience, and mated his dog with one of the same strain, thereby strengthening the probability of the puppies being in their turn likely to beget good-headed offspring when allied with another strain of blood, he would, in the course of a few years, have most probably got exactly the sort of dog he desired to obtain. We are perfectly aware that this argument may be said to cut both ways, and that those taking a contrary view of the case to our own may exclaim that the faults are just as likely to be perpetuated as the good properties; but we would observe that perpetual wandering from one blood to another *must* eventually produce specimens of uncertain type, whose services at the stud are perfectly useless from the fact that there is no fixed character in their breeding, and who are liable to throw puppies of every conceivable shape and make in the same litter. In short, in-breeding is, when judiciously carried out, absolutely essential to a breeder's success as a breeder, if such is to be maintained.

Finally, before closing our remarks upon the general subject of breeding, we wish to warn beginners that they are undertaking a tedious and very disappointing pursuit when they set up to be breeders of exhibition dogs. The best of calculations are often upset by accident or fate, and many a promising puppy falls a victim to the ills that puppyhood is peculiarly heir to. To have bred a first-rate dog of any breed is indeed a thing to be proud of, when it is considered how many scores of persons are expending time and money and judgment upon this very object. How few champions there are in the world is a statement which can be read in two ways—either there are so few that it should be an easy matter to add to their number ; or it may be construed as implying that a vast amount of labour is wasted in trying to produce what is in reality a matter of chance. To us there appears to be both truth and untruth in each opinion ; but the fact remains that champions have arisen, and will arise again, and are far more likely to be brought into existence when due attention is paid to the mates a breeder selects for his dogs.

Careful people invariably keep regular stud books referring to their breeding operations ; in these the date of birth (and if necessary of the purchase), colour, sex, weight, breeder, and performances of their stock, are registered. The visits of their own bitches, and of others to their stud dogs, are also entered ; as are the dates of sales, and the names and addresses of the purchasers. By this means ready and accurate information can be obtained concerning the history of any animal which may at one time or other pass through their hands.

THE STUD DOG.

A great deal of a breeder's success depends upon the state of health in which the stud dog is when he begets offspring ; for a delicate or unhealthy dog is more than likely to transmit his defects to his puppies, who are in consequence more difficult to rear, and of less value when they attain maturity. Considerable attention should therefore be paid to the comfort of a dog who is in the habit of receiving a large number of stud visits. He should, if possible, be well exercised morning and evening, either by a country walk, or a run round his owner's yard ; and his diet must be wholesome and liberal. A plunge in cold water materially assists in keeping a dog in vigorous condition, and in warm weather may be taken daily. It should be borne in mind, too, that it is always well to have your stud dogs look clean and tidy, both when out of doors and when in the kennels. Much depends upon the first impressions formed by the owner of a bitch who contemplates breeding from him, and many a dog is passed over whose services, had he been in better fettle, might have been resorted to. Care should be taken not to overtax the energies of a young sire by allowing him to receive too many stud visits ; the result of excesses in this way being both sickly offspring and his own ultimate failure at the stud. Fifteen or twenty bitches a year are quite enough for a dog not in his prime, and about twice the number for a dog in the full vigour of his strength. As a rule, dogs under eighteen months old are not likely to do themselves or their owners much good if bred from ; and availing one's self of the services of a very old dog is always risky. It is extremely hard to state an age at which a dog can be said to be "old" ; some retain the vigour of their youth up to ten years and more, whilst others get decrepit and break up at six or seven. So much depends upon constitution and careful attendance, that it is impossible to advise upon the age at which a stud dog ceases to be of use ; but breeders should see the dog for themselves, if they do not know him, and judge, from his appearance and condition, whether he is likely to suit their wishes.

On the arrival of a bitch for service, the owner of the stud dog should, unless time is a matter of consideration, fasten her up securely, and let her recover from the fatigues of her journey before the introduction takes place. A night's rest and a feed are very likely to assist nature's course, a bitch served immediately after a tiring journey being far more likely to miss conception than one who has rested and become a little accustomed to the place and those around her. Many bitches are very troublesome and restive when with the dog, and throw themselves about in a most violent manner; others are savage and morose, and if not carefully looked after are likely to fly at him and perhaps do some serious injury. In such cases the bitch must be held by the collar, but care should be taken that she does not get half suffocated by too tight a grasp being placed on it. The possibility of a fight taking place, or of the dog requiring some assistance, especially in the case of young bitches, make it undesirable that the pair should be left alone together for any length of time, much less after connection is terminated.

After union it is some time before the animals can be separated: twenty minutes is about the average, though, of course, this period is often exceeded or decreased in duration. After that the breeder must wait patiently for Nature to take its course, when the bitch should be kenneled by herself on straw, and kept as quiet as possible. It is desirable that a second visit should, if possible, be paid after an interval of thirty-six or forty-eight hours. The majority of the owners of stud dogs gladly consent to this arrangement, as it lessens the chances of the bitch proving barren, and also saves them trouble, and their dog from getting a bad name as a stock-getter.

A sire should be looked upon with suspicion if his services are in too great request, and the number of his receptions unlimited, as it is only reasonable to expect sickly offspring from a dog whose stud experiences are practically unrestricted. A very old dog, unless mated to a young and vigorous bitch, is more than likely to fail to beget stock at all: and if he succeeds in doing so, the puppies are very frequently of bad constitution and delicate in their earlier days. It is often the case that the services of a successful show dog are most eagerly sought after by breeders, and the merits of his *father* entirely overlooked; and this is certainly a fact which must puzzle all practical men when they reflect upon it. A sire of good pedigree, who can produce stock of superior quality to himself, is better worth patronising at a low fee than his successful son who has yet to prove himself the success at the stud which he is on the bench or in the field; especially as in the latter instance the sum charged for his services is sure to be a considerable one. Many of our champion dogs have turned out complete failures from a breeder's point of view; whilst their plainer-looking fathers or brothers have begotten offspring of a far better stamp, though with only half the chances of success. A golden rule in dog-breeding is, for the owner to satisfy himself that his bitch *really does* visit the dog he has selected for her. In many instances we know tricks to have been played upon owners who have sent their bitches to dogs at a distance; and we have ourselves been applied to for the services of a dog, standing at a low fee, by an owner of a stud dog, for a bitch sent up to the latter. Unfortunately, in ignorance of the fact, we granted his request, and only afterwards discovered what had occurred, and that the bitch, the name of whose owner we never ascertained, had been sent up to this gentleman's dog, and was not one of his own. The difference between the fees of the two dogs was three guineas; and as it was impossible for us to *prove* that the owner was not informed of what took place, we were unable to take steps in the matter, and our acquaintance still walks the streets an honest man. If the distance is too far to accompany the bitch or send one's man, it is a very good plan to get a friend in the neighbourhood of the stud dog's kennel to accompany her when she visits him, especially in dealing with strangers. Of course, in the case of owners whose characters are above suspicion these precautions are unnecessary; but it will always be a satisfaction to the proprietor of a stud dog to know that the bitch's visit has been witnessed by her owner or his nominee, especially if she should fail to be in pup. In event of the latter being the case, the usual practice is that the same bitch may visit the dog a second time gratuitously, or another of the same owner's at half price; but here again caution must be exercised on the part of the proprietor of the stud dog, for instances have occurred when puppies have been born dead, and he has been told there was no result from the union of the parents. Owners of stud dogs often do, and always should, provide the owners of bitches which have visited them with formal certificates of service; such documents are particularly useful in event of disputed pedigrees.

THE BROOD BITCH.

Young bitches often exhibit symptoms of an inclination to breed at the age of eight or nine months, but it is undesirable to place them at the stud until they have reached the age of at least eighteen months. The remarks we made above against the advisability of resorting to the services of too young a sire, apply with even greater force when a youthful bitch is under consideration. Stunted and puny puppies are almost sure to be produced from a young mother; and the injury they are likely to do her constitution is incalculable. It must be borne in mind that for weeks before birth her system is sorely taxed to provide them with nourishment, and after the shock of labour is gone through there is a further strain upon her until they are weaned.

The first symptom afforded by a bitch that she is likely to be soon ready for breeding purposes, is a desire on her part to romp and play with any dog she meets. This may possibly arise from merely exuberance of spirits, but it is always well to keep a close eye upon her as soon as any undue levity is observed in her conduct. It is most desirable to use every endeavour to keep the animal away from all risk of being got at by strange dogs; and when the matter is placed beyond doubt all former precautions should be doubled if possible. It must be remembered that there is not only a great risk of dogs getting into the place where the bitch is confined, but that she will probably be equally anxious to escape from her kennel, and some bitches have performed almost incredible feats in their endeavours to do so.

She should, if at a distance, be sent off to the kennels where the dog is standing a day or two after the earlier symptoms appear, so as to be in time. If despatched by public conveyance, it is imperative that she be securely confined in a box or basket from which escape is impossible. The transit of dogs has been more fully treated in the chapter on exhibiting, and need not be further alluded to here; but all breeders should be impressed with the absolute necessity of exercising the greatest vigilance when they have bitches by them under such circumstances. For at least a week after the bitch has visited the dog, the precautions for isolating her must not be relaxed, or all her owner's hopes may be marred by her forming a connection with a stranger.

The influence of a previous sire on a subsequent litter of puppies is a subject of the keenest discussion and interest amongst breeders, and a most interesting correspondence has taken place in the columns of the *Live Stock Journal* relating thereto. Some of the statements which have appeared from time to time in that journal upon this subject, and which have been substantiated by the names of writers whose position as breeders of various varieties of live stock is assured, are invested with a peculiar importance. But having carefully read and considered the matter, we find ourselves driven back on the supposition that although such occurrences undoubtedly have arisen, they are not by any means the matter-of-course events some of the correspondents of the *Live Stock Journal* consider them, and in more than one instance we have failed to satisfy ourselves that the influences imputed have regulated the course

THE BROOD BITCH.

of events. In making this statement we attribute to the writers no desire to impose on public credulity, but we think they have too often forgotten the influence which surrounding objects exercise over the mind of a pregnant female. This opinion is shared by many breeders of live stock, and it is notorious that a celebrated breeder of black polled cattle had his premises and fences tarred, with the express object of assisting Nature in keeping the colour of his stock as deep as possible. It is, however, quite impossible for us to go at length into the subject, and it must therefore be dismissed with the remark that as many breeders firmly believe, from personal experience, that such a thing as past influence is possible, especially in the case of maiden bitches, due vigilance should be exercised in the thorough isolation of bitches when in season, or more than a temporary evil and disappointment may occur

PUPPING.

Having selected a proper mate for his bitch, and sent her to him, all anxiety is removed from an owner's mind for some time at least ; for during the first period of going with young, the bitch will require no special diet or attention. It may be here stated, for the benefit of the uninitiated, that the period of gestation amongst dogs is sixty-three days, and that this time is rarely exceeded unless something is wrong, though it sometimes occurs that the whelps make their appearance some days before they are expected. During this period the bitch should be allowed plenty of exercise, but during the latter portion of her pregnancy she is peculiarly liable to chills ; every care should therefore be taken to avoid any risk of her taking cold, and all washing operations and *violent* exercise must then be suspended. Our own experience has taught us that in the majority of instances it is almost impossible to tell whether or no the bitch is in whelp until the third or fourth week, and on many occasions we have known breeders to be in doubt for a much longer period ; in fact, on discussing with a very well-known Pointer exhibitor the accouchement of one of his exhibits during a show, he assured us that when she left home she had shown no traces of being in whelp, and as a matter of fact her time was not up until the following week.

A week or so before the date on which it is expected that she will whelp, the bitch should be installed in the quarters in which it is arranged the interesting event is to take place. The reason for this is that dogs must get used to a kennel before they will make themselves at home in it, and this feeling is peculiarly perceptible in the case of a bitch who has recently whelped ; for in many cases she will try and carry her puppies (greatly to the damage of the latter) back to her old quarters rather than let them remain in a kennel to which she is unaccustomed. Having got her reconciled to her change of abode, the *locale* of which should, if possible, be away from the other dogs, so as to let her have more quiet (but *warmth* and *absence of draught* are even more essential than isolation in such cases), and supposing the time of her whelping to be near at hand, it is desirable that the bitch should be provided with a diet of a more strengthening character than that which she has been in the habit of receiving. This need not consist entirely of meat or other heating foods, which can only tend to increase her discomfort in parturition, but may be made of scraps well boiled or stewed, with the addition of bread, meal, or rice, which in their turn will absorb the gravy or soup, and form, in conjunction with the scraps, when the latter are chopped up, a meal which is both wholesome and nutritious. A few days before the puppies make their appearance a considerable change is usually perceptible in the bitch ; the presence of milk can be detected, and a considerable enlargement of the stomach takes place. Her behaviour too, clearly indicates that she is uneasy and in pain, and in many instances the appetite entirely fails, and the bowels become confined. In the latter case a mild purgative of either castor, linseed, or sweet oil must be given. The first-named remedy is sometimes too powerful an aperient for a bitch in such a condition, as, in the more delicate breeds especially, it is apt to cause severe straining, which would injure the puppies. Before resorting, therefore, to castor-oil, an experimental dose of either linseed or sweet oil might be administered, which, if it succeed in acting on the bowels, will have satisfactorily accomplished the owner's object; and as the lubricating power of all three oils is essentially the same, the internal organs will be equally benefited by either medicine.

Two or three days before the puppies are due a good bed of straw should be provided, and this should not be changed till the whelps are at least a week old; for unnecessary attention will certainly worry the mother, and may cause her to destroy her offspring. The bed of straw should be placed on boards raised not higher than two or three inches from the ground; in fact, the bitch during the last few weeks of going in whelp should not be allowed the opportunity of leaping up and down on and off a high bench. On no account should the bed be placed on a cold stone or brick flooring; and even a carpet is objectionable, for the mother, in making her bed for the reception of her young, invariably removes all the bedding from underneath her, and piles it up at the sides in the shape of a nest. Her object in acting thus is to facilitate the operation of licking the puppies; as she will within a few hours of parturition have all her whelps thoroughly cleansed and freed from any offensive adherent matter, being during their earlier puppyhood most attentive to the personal cleanliness of her offspring. This would be impossible if she allowed them to lie on the straw, as the wet would soak into it and cause the bed to become foul.

The different temperaments and dispositions of various bitches become specially apparent as parturition approaches. Some will be impatient at the slightest intrusion on the solitude they evidently prefer, whilst others eagerly welcome the familiar voice of master or attendant, and seem to beg him to remain beside them in the time of suffering. A great deal must therefore be left to the judgment of those in charge of the bitch; but it should be borne in mind that, though an occasional visit is necessary even in the case of a most unsociably-disposed bitch, in order to see that nothing has gone wrong, still *too much* interference and fidgeting even with a quiet one is apt to render her feverish, and increase the difficulties of her situation. Under any circumstances a plentiful amount of cold water should always be placed near her, and beyond this she will, in the majority of instances, want nothing until the pups are born. Should she however become exhausted during labour, a little port wine may be given now and then. When safely delivered, some gruel should be given her, and she should be kept on this diet for the space of two or three days; it is strengthening and soothing to the internal organs, and can be made either with milk or water; the addition of a little gravy or beef tea is an excellent practice after the first two or three basins of gruel. The quantity of gruel should be unlimited, and very often she will devour a basinful every two or three hours for the first day; care, however, must be taken not to let it remain by her too long, so as to turn sour and disarrange the stomach, which it is very easy to do when a bitch has just whelped. It is always desirable to try and count the puppies when the mother is off the bed feeding, as it lets an owner know whether she eats her whelps or not; and if he misses puppies he must try and devise some way to stop the proceeding.

In event of a puppy dying, it must of course be removed at the first opportunity offering itself, and if this can be managed without the knowledge of the mother, so much the better; for we have known instances where a whole litter has been destroyed by a dam on the removal of one dead whelp from their midst; and, besides this, there is the danger of a bite from a bad-tempered bitch if she sees her family carried off. Opinions vary much as regards whether dogs can count or not; but our own belief is decidedly in favour of their being able to do so up to a certain number. This is a matter of considerable importance where puppies are concerned, for it is often necessary to remove some from the mother. Some bitches seem to take no notice of the diminished number of their family, whilst others appear frenzied by their bereavement, and, acting on a first impulse, have destroyed the remaining whelps, unless restrained from doing so. It being therefore certain that mothers are capable of discovering, by counting or otherwise, when any of their puppies have been removed in their absence, it behoves the breeder to be careful how he acts when such a course has to be adopted. If he carefully watches the bitch for half an hour or so on her re-introduction to her family, and sees that all is well, he need have no further care on that score; but should she become restless, and show signs of an inclination to destroy the remaining whelps, she must be closely guarded in order to prevent mischief. Some bitches are notorious for the habit they have of killing their puppies, and in such cases the only means to adopt is, in the absence of a foster-mother, to take the puppies in-doors, and keep them warmly wrapped up in a basket lined with flannel before a fire, and let the mother come and suckle them every two hours. Whilst with them she should be laid on her side, and gently held down so as to prevent her injuring them in any way.

Having alluded above to the subject of foster-mothers, we may express the opinion that, in the event of valuable puppies being expected, the acquisition of such an animal is very desirable. A bitch in whelp can often be obtained from the Dogs' Home, Battersea, for a few shillings, and if one is not to be obtained there in a suitable condition of pregnancy, Mr. Scorborio, the courteous and energetic manager of that institution can often put owners in the way of obtaining one at a very reasonable figure. Foster-mothers can also frequently be hired for a few weeks, if advertised for in the papers; and as a matter of fact we once obtained the services of seven at £1 each from one advertisement in the *Live Stock Journal*. The greatest precaution must however be exercised by owners, in order that no diseased or unhealthy bitch be received in the responsible position of wet-nurse to their puppies, for the danger of such an introduction can hardly be exaggerated; and therefore many persons rather shrink from investing in bitches of whose antecedents they are ignorant.

Aid from inexperienced persons when administered to a bitch in labour is almost sure to be attended with most unsatisfactory results, and we are simply re-echoing the opinion of the vast majority of practical breeders when we express the conviction that many of the so-called veterinary surgeons practising in this country know next to nothing of canine pathology. A man who may or may not have passed his examination at the Veterinary College, and professes to be an adept at physicking horses or doctoring cows, invariably considers himself quite qualified to attend upon dogs, and possibly in a few cases he may be so; but in most instances he knows less than the kennel-man does, and increases the ailing dog's difficulties by his injudicious treatment. "There is a man down the street who knows all about dogs," is a common saying when the owner is in a difficulty, and the man is sent for, generally turning out to be absolutely incompetent and grossly ignorant of what he professes to understand. For our own part we believe that doctoring their own dogs is an easy task for tolerably intelligent and fairly attentive owners, and experience has taught us that the list of drugs and remedies which are applicable to canine diseases is a very limited one indeed, and that an elaborate doggy pharmacopœia is a wholly unnecessary institution, which can only tend to complicate the difficulties which lie in the way of a beginner when he attempts to arrive at a correct diagnosis and treatment of his animal's ailments. In cases of protracted labour, where there are indications of internal complications, surgical aid must of course be rendered the bitch, provided really competent professional assistance can be obtained. All other is useless in such cases, and we must once again impress upon our readers the terrible danger and torture to which they subject their dogs by calling in the assistance of incompetent advisers. *Be convinced that your surgeon knows more than you do yourself*, is a golden rule for breeders to lay heed to.

In the event of the bitch being unable to pass her puppies after being in labour for some time, the application of crushed ice to the abdomen is frequently the means of enabling her to do so, as it has the effect of contracting the muscles of the womb, and thus assists in the expulsion of the whelps. Ergot is sometimes used in complicated cases as a uterine excitant, but should be resorted to only as an extreme measure, being, in the hands of inexperienced persons, a very dangerous medicine. Oiling the vagina is also in many cases a relief to the bitch. In some books we have seen it strongly recommended as a means of assisting protracted labour that the bitch should be immersed in a warm bath for a few minutes; this in ninety-nine cases out of a hundred involves two certain results—(1) almost instant relief to the dog, (2) DEATH. According to the theory propounded by Mayhew in his work on canine diseases, the application of warm water causes a relaxation of the muscles of the womb, whereas an exactly opposite effect is needed; thus the temporary relief from her suffering costs the poor beast her life, and her owner the mortification of having killed her by improper treatment. We know not of one only, but of scores of such instances occurring; and no doubt all breeders of experience are well acquainted with the ill effects of an injudicious bath to a bitch in labour.

Some curiosity on the part of a youthful breeder is natural enough where the first puppies of his own breeding are concerned; but he will be acting very foolishly indeed if he gives way to it. It cannot be any advantage to him to discover the sexes of the different whelps on the day of their birth, and all handling should be avoided unless it is thought desirable to remove some from the mother on account of the number being considered too many for her to bring up. It should be borne in mind that four or five strong, vigorous, well-nourished puppies are far more likely to turn out satisfactorily for their owner than eight or ten scantily-nourished ones; and it must be left to the good sense of the breeder to decide, from the condition of the bitch and the amount of milk she has secreted, how many she can do justice to without injuring herself. Five or six are enough for a moderate-sized bitch, and eight or ten for a large one. The extra ones can be destroyed if sickly, or placed under a foster-mother, if one can be got. In some instances puppies have been very successfully brought up by hand, through the immediate agency of a baby's feeding bottle; but before any one enters upon such an undertaking due consideration should be devoted to the magnitude of the task before him. Constant feeding is necessary, and the whelps require a great deal of warmth, patience, and attention. In circumstances like this the most valuable ally of all is to be found in the cook; if her hearty co-operation is obtained the chances are that the whelps will go on and prosper, for a snug corner for the basket on the kitchen hearth, and the constant supervision she can give them, is sure to benefit them very considerably.

About the ninth day the puppies begin to open their eyes, and very soon they commence crawling out of their nest and about the floor of the kennel; after which it is wonderful how fast they seem to grow and the strength they display. At two weeks old they will commence to eat bread-and-gravy, or bread-and-milk, if it is provided for them, though the latter is, we think, an objectionable diet, as it is apt to turn sour, and also, if cow's milk, to breed worms, to which young puppies are peculiarly liable. Goat's milk, however, we consider good for puppies, as it, according to our experience, does not increase the risk of worms. During this time the food given to the mother should be of a strengthening nature, so as to enable her to stand the strain on her constitution which her maternal duties involve, but care should be taken to prevent her bringing bones into her bed, as many instances have occurred of mothers severely biting their puppies who have attempted to take the bones from her. One or two gentle runs a day are now very necessary for the bitch, as exercise not only freshens her considerably, but gives her a chance of getting away from the persistent persecution which the puppies inflict upon her. At five weeks old the whelps may usually begin to be removed from their mother, and it is well to do this gradually, as they suffer less from the separation if this course is pursued; and by extending the intervals of the bitch's absence they can be almost entirely weaned without any ill effects to either themselves or their dam. The best method is to begin by removing the bitch for an hour or two in the warmest part of the day, so that the chance of the puppies catching cold is diminished. The periods of her absence can then be prolonged until she is only returned to them of a night, and finally ceases to visit them at all.

It frequently occurs that the teats of the bitch have been wounded by the teeth of the puppies when they suckle her; and inflammation, from the influx of milk, often arises when they are removed. Considerable relief can be obtained by rubbing some camphorated oil well over her stomach, and this can be repeated night and morning for some days, a mild dose of physic being administered when the puppies are finally removed. In the event, however, of the milk that she has secreted still bothering her, and her teats being so tender that drawing some off by ordinary milking is impossible recourse may be had to an ordinary soda-water bottle, heated with hot water, the mouth of which can be pressed over the inflamed teat. This has the effect of drawing some of the milk out, and thereby relieving the bitch of a great deal of pain. Or an ordinary breast-pump may be employed.

Having now given a brief sketch of the general treatment of a bitch when pupping, we will pass on to the future management of the whelps themselves.

REARING.

On the removal of the whelps from their mother, a very considerable change for the worse immediately takes place in their appearance, which is due mainly to the alteration in their diet and general mode of life. Instead of drawing a certain amount of sustenance from their dam at the cost of no trouble, they are now cast upon their own resources for a means of subsistence. The necessity of having to get up and hunt about for the dish which contains its food is a fact which it takes a puppy's mind a long time to master. Consequently the entire litter often passes many hungry hours during the night, although their food is within a few inches of their bed; and it is not until a happy thought strikes one of them that it might be a good plan if he got up and looked for something, that they all follow his example, and fall to as only hungry puppies can. Almost all puppies suffer greatly from worms, and immediately on their removal from their mother means should be taken to rid them of such torments. The presence of worms is certain when the stomachs of puppies swell and harden, but they frequently exist without developing such symptoms. It is therefore the safer plan to administer one or two doses of worm medicine all round, especial care being taken that their delicate mouths and throats are not injured in administering the remedy. The two best vermifuges are areca-nut and santonine. The latter, in its crystallised form, is an excellent remedy for worms in dogs, and about two grains in butter cannot be surpassed as a vermifuge for puppies of seven or eight weeks old, whose parents weigh from forty to sixty pounds weight. If too strong a dose is given, santonine has a tendency to affect the brain and cause fits, so precaution must be exercised in administering this medicine. The chief difficulty in the use of areca-nut lies in getting it freshly grated, as if allowed to become stale it loses its virtue as an anthelmintic. To avoid this the nut should be grated on an ordinary nutmeg-grater, and given immediately in butter or lard. The ordinary dose is two grains for every pound the dog weighs, but more than two drachms should never be given. Spratt's worm powders are also excellent remedies, if an owner has to clear his pets of these pests, and are easily procured of any chemist.

It is useless to resort to any remedy for worms in dogs unless the medicine is administered on an empty stomach. Small dogs should fast for at least twelve hours, and large powerful animals for twenty-four, before the medicine is administered. It is also desirable to prevent their drinking too much water during the period of their abstention, the object being to deprive the worms of all sorts of food, so that the anthelmintic may have a greater chance of success. Many persons give a dose of castor-oil the night before the vermifuge is given, and a second one two or three hours after if it has had no effect. As long as the purgative does not tax the dog's system too powerfully, these precautions materially assist the operation of the medicine; but judgment and caution must, of course, be exercised, and it would be foolish to adopt such vigorous treatment with a weakly puppy.

Crushed biscuits, oatmeal-porridge, and bread-and-gravy, with the addition of a little chopped meat and vegetables, are the best diet for puppies when first away from their mother, and the amount they can get through in the course of twenty-four hours is considerable. The greatest care must be taken to guard against the puppies (this, in fact, applies to any dogs, but to puppies especially) being given food which is *sour or decomposed.* A very fruitful and common cause of this has only lately come to our knowledge. We are indebted for the following information to Mr. F. Gresham, whose experience in feeding large dogs is very considerable. This gentleman has proved by experience that food cooked in a copper or other boiler is very apt to turn sour as soon as cooked, if allowed to stand and cool *in the vessel in which it has been prepared.* Care should therefore be taken to remove it, as soon as the culinary operations are completed, to a cool and clean receptacle, where it can remain until it is required for the dogs, or is returned to the boiler, to be added to other meals in course of preparation.

All draughts should be kept away from their kennel, which must be warm and dry, or the puppies will not spread and grow as they should do; and a run in a dry yard is imperative, if the weather is not too cold or damp. By keeping his puppies clean and dry, an owner considerably lessens the risk of distemper ravaging his kennels, for this fearful scourge is unquestionably amenable to sanitary arrangements, and except on very rare occasions, when its origin can usually be traced, is scarcely ever present in well-conducted establishments. In our own kennels we have never experienced a single case of distemper amongst puppies of our own breeding, and this has been under circumstances of great difficulty, where for over three years an average of nearly fifty dogs have been kept in confined spaces. A strict attention to cleanliness, fresh air, fresh water, sound food, combined with proper grooming and exercise, renders the presence of distemper well-nigh impossible, and if a breeder who attends to these matters has the misfortune to have it communicated to his stock (for distemper *is* contagious), he will find them the better able to resist its attacks if they have been previously well looked after.

Our own treatment in the few cases we had in cases of puppies we had bought (one or two of which sickened within the week) were thorough and absolute isolation in the first place, so as to preclude all possibility of contagion or infection in case of other diseases. We had a lumber-room attached to the house cleared for a hospital, and fitted with a gas stove; by this means a steady even temperature can be maintained night and day, and this is a most important feature in the treatment of distemper. All stuffiness in the air should be avoided, for it must be remembered that in this disease the nostrils become charged with a thick fluid which renders breathing very difficult. We invariably had the window open at the top, and with the gas stove aided by a thermometer kept the room at a steady temperature of 60 degrees. The only food given was beef-tea with some bread soaked in it, and the only medicine Rackham's distemper pills. Seeing is believing, and we believe these pills to be almost infallible in the treatment of distemper, never having lost a dog when using them, and knowing many breeders who share our opinion, we cannot resist alluding to them. When the graver symptoms begin to subside solid food can be administered, and the dog picks up wonderfully soon, though too premature an introduction to the cold outside is to be deprecated after his confinement so long in a warm temperature. A friend—we rather think it was Mr. R. Fulton, of Brockley—once told us of a food which he considered a capital change for dogs suffering from distemper, and this was a number of fresh haddocks' heads put into a pot and covered with water, to be boiled until the bones of the fish get soft and the water is almost entirely absorbed; this, when cold, forms a jelly, which is keenly appreciated by the invalids, and seems to do them good. Our friend's theory was that the phosphorus contained in the fish-bones assisted the medicine in curing the dog; but be this as it may, it is certain that no ill effects, but rather the contrary, resulted from giving it them.

Allusion having thus been made to the two greatest plagues of puppyhood—worms and distemper—there hardly remain more diseases to which they are peculiarly liable. Fits they certainly often suffer from, but these almost invariably are the result of worms, and will subside and disappear when the irritating cause of their presence is removed. Teething occasionally troubles them, but seldom to any great extent, for puppies do not usually shed their first teeth until nine months old, and then they are strong enough to bear the pain and annoyance the cutting of their new ones inflicts upon them. Should the puppies, however, appear to suffer from the swelling of their gums previous to the appearance of a tooth, it is well to lance the inflamed part, especially if the gum appears abnormally hard. Not only does this give immediate relief, but it helps the teeth to come up in a regular line, which in most varieties is most desirable.

The exercise and subsequent treatment of the whelps have been so thoroughly gone into in the chapters on general management and exercise, that no further allusion to them is requisite here.

MELOX

ADMITTED TO BE THE
FINEST DOG FOOD IN EXISTENCE!

Improves and Strengthens the Digestive Organs, Gives Gloss to the Coat, Muscle to the Body

And from which is obtained the greatest results ever experienced in the Canine World.

Can be obtained of all Local Tradesmen.

Prices: 1-cwt. bags. 20/- ½-cwt. bags. 10/- ¼-cwt. bags. 5/2 14-lb. bags. 2/8 7-lb. bags. 1/4½ 5-lb. bags. 1/-

Each Bag is sealed. Carriage Paid on ½-cwt. quantities and upwards.

A 5-lb. Bag sent free per parcels post 1/7.

MELOX MARVELS
The New Dry Diet for Dogs.

A Dainty Miniature Biscuit weighing about 250 to the lb.

Possessing great nourishment and recommended where a dry diet is preferred or as a change from other foods.

Prices: 1-cwt. bags. 21/- ½-cwt. bags. 10/6 ¼-cwt. bags. 5/4 14-lb. bags. 2/9 7-lb. bags. 1/5

Carriage paid on ½-cwt. quantities and upwards.
A sample 7-lb. bag free per parcels post 2/-.

BUFFALO PUPPY CAKES & BUFFALO TERRIER CAKES

Are specially adapted for use with above, where a change of Diet or Dry Food is required. **SAMPLES POST FREE.**

CLARKES' BISCUIT FACTORY, LIMEHOUSE, LONDON, E.
By Special Warrant to **HIS MAJESTY THE KING.**

BEWARE OF LOW-PRICED IMITATIONS.
BENBOW'S

REGISTERED TRADE MARK.
DOG MIXTURE.
Established over 60 Years.
THE ORIGINAL MEDICINE. THE RELIABLE TONIC.
Acknowledged by Owners, Trainers, and Breeders the best Medicine for the Cure of
Distemper, Jaundice, Preventing Worms, &c.
It will be found most efficacious for
DOGS FOR EXHIBITION
As, by a course of treatment during preparation,
PERFECT CONDITION can be assured together with a sleekness of coat so essential for success on the Show Bench.

Testimonials enclosed with each bottle from successful Exhibitors, and from
Over 30 WINNERS of the WATERLOO CUP.

Sold in Bottles **2/-, 5/-,** & **10/-** each ; and in **1** gall. Tins for the use of Kennels, **45/-** each ; also in Capsules, in Boxes containing **40** Quarter-Teaspoonfuls, **24** Half Teaspoonfuls, or **15** Teaspoonfuls, **2/6** each.

Benbow's Medicated Dog Soap
(Non-Mercurial).
Thoroughly cleanses the Skin, removing all insects, Price **6d.** per Tablet.
Of all Chemists and Druggists everywhere.
Sole Proprietors—
BENBOW'S DOG MIXTURE CO.,
181, ALDERSGATE STREET, LONDON, E.C.

a

LACTOL

—— FOR ——

Weaning and Rearing Puppies and Kittens.

**NO COOKING REQUIRED—JUST ADD HOT WATER.
HUNDREDS OF UNSOLICITED TESTIMONIALS RECEIVED.
USED IN ALL THE LEADING KENNELS.**

THE most critical stage of a puppy's existence is the weaning period—from five to eight weeks old—when he is taken from the dam. Until the introduction of Lactol, puppies, as a general rule, were weaned on unsuitable foods, most unlike the mother's milk that they have but shortly left, with the result that they invariably suffered from indigestion, diarrhœa, vomiting, distended stomach, &c., and in many cases died.

An analysis of the milk of a bitch shows immediately why this should be the case, as it is seen to be three times as strong as cow's or goat's milk. The only food on which puppies can be safely weaned and reared is Lactol, which, when mixed with hot water as directed, forms a food three times as strong as cow's milk, and identical in taste, analysis, and appearance with the puppy's natural food.

It is regularly used and recommended by all the leading dog fanciers and canine specialists, and is most highly spoken of by the veterinary and kennel press.

In Tins, 1/-, 2/6, 5/- and 20/-.

Of BOOTS', TAYLOR'S DRUG CO., WHITELEY'S, HARRODS, ARMY & NAVY STORES, and other leading Stores and Chemists, or from the Manufacturers :—

A. F. SHERLEY & CO., 46 & 48, BOROUGH HIGH ST., S.E.

HYGIENIC, WARM and COMFORTABLE

NON-IRRITATING and INEXPENSIVE.

for HEALTH & COMFORT in the KENNEL.

Sole Makers—
CITY OF LONDON WOOD-WOOL Co.,
Contractors to H.M. Government,
Plover Street, Gainsboro' Road, Victoria Park, London, N.E.

TWENTY YEARS A BREEDER AND EXHIBITOR

VISITORS TO MR. WINTON SMITH'S 'KENNELS, at THE BEECHES, BOREHAM WOOD, HERTS. (under a mile from Elstree Station, M.R., and thirty minutes' by rail from St. Pancras) will always find a large selection of all breeds of SPANIELS, NO-SLIP RETRIEVERS, POINTERS, and SETTERS, several of which are Field Trial and Show Bench Winners. They can be tried on the premises, and will be sold, conditionally they can be exchanged if found unsatisfactory, or they will be sent on trial on the usual terms. TERRIERS in variety for companions, sport, or exhibition. STUD DOGS (winners and workers). BROOD BITCHES and PUPPIES (latter at walk). Any other breeds procured for home or exportation. Shipments personally conducted. Full particulars on application. *National Telephone,* 3 *Elstree.*

SECOND-HAND BOOKS AT HALF PRICES !!

New Books at 25 per cent. Discount.

Books on Poultry, Gardening, Farming, Technical, Educational, Medical, Law, Theological, all other Subjects, and for all Examinations (Elementary and Advanced) supplied.

State Wants.   Send for Catalogue No. 7.
Books Sent on Approval.
BOOKS BOUGHT.   BEST PRICES GIVEN.

W. & G. FOYLE,
135, Charing Cross Rd., LONDON, W.C.

WE MANUFACTURE
KENNELS AND KENNEL APPLIANCES
of every description.

No. 108.—DOUBLE KENNELS WITH COVERED RUNS.
For Terriers, Bulldogs, etc.

Each kennel 4ft. by 3ft., and each run 5ft. by 4ft., 3ft. 6in. high at eaves, 5ft. to ridge. Walls of rustic jointed boards, wood slab roof painted. Kennels fitted with raised benches and boarded floor. Wood partitions to runs.

CASH PRICE for Double Kennels, as illustrated £8 15 0
Larger size for Retrievers 13 10 0

No. 93.—NEW REGISTERED DOG KENNEL.

Made of best red deal, thoroughly seasoned and highly finished. Bench slides under kennel when not in use. Folding inside partition, ensuring warm and dry bed in all weathers. Front opens in two halves for cleaning purposes. Can be taken to pieces and packed flat for travelling.

CASH PRICES.
For Terriers... ... £1 3 6
 ,, Bulldogs ... 1 10 0
 ,, Collies 1 16 0
 ,, St. Bernards ... 3 0 0

Carriage paid on all orders of 40/- value and upwards.

NOTE.—All our Kennels are thoroughly finished before leaving works, and only selected material is used in the manufacture.

Write for Illustrated Catalogue.

BOULTON & PAUL, L^TD.
Department C., NORWICH.

Established over a Century.

The Kennel Library.

BRITISH DOGS.
Their Points, Selection, and Show Preparation. Third Edition. By eminent specialists. Beautifully Illustrated. This is the fullest work on the various breeds of dogs kept in England. In one volume, *demy 8vo, cloth, price 12/6 nett, by post 13/-.*

PRACTICAL KENNEL MANAGEMENT.
A Complete Treatise on the Proper Management of Dogs, for the Show Bench, the Field, or as Companions, with a chapter on Diseases—their Causes and Treatment. By well-known Specialists. Illustrated. *In cloth, price 10/6 nett, by post 11/-.*

DISEASES OF DOGS.
Their Causes, Symptoms, and Treatment; Modes of Administering Medicines; Treatment in cases of Poisoning, &c. For the use of Amateurs. By HUGH DALZIEL. Fourth Edition. Entirely Re-written and brought up to date. By ALEX. C. PIESSE, M.R.C.V.S. *Price 1/- nett, by post 1/2; in cloth, price 2/- nett, by post 2/3.*

BREAKING AND TRAINING DOGS.
Being Concise Directions for the proper education of Dogs, both for the Field and for Companions. Second Edition. By " PATHFINDER." Many new Illustrations. *In cloth, price 6/6 nett, by post 6/10.*

POPULAR DOG KEEPING:
Being a Handy Guide to the General Management and Training of all Kinds of Dogs for Companions and Pets. Third Edition. By J. MAXTEE. Illustrated. *Price 1/- nett, by post 1/2.*

THE FOX TERRIER.
Its Points, Breeding, Rearing, Preparing for Exhibition. Second Edition, Revised and brought up to date. Fully Illustrated. *Price 1/- nett, by post 1/2.*

THE COLLIE,
As a Show Dog, Companion, and Worker. Revised by J. MAXTEE. Third Edition. Illustrated. *Price 1/- nett, by post 1/2.*

THE GREYHOUND:
Its Points, Breeding, Rearing, Training, and Running. Second Edition, Revised and brought up to date by J. MAXTEE, assisted by T. B. RIXON. Illustrated. *Price 1/- nett, by post 1/2.*

THE WHIPPET OR RACE-DOG.
How to Breed, Rear, Train, Race, and Exhibit the Whippet, the Management of Race Meetings, and Original Plans of Courses. By FREEMAN LLOYD. Illustrated. *Price 1/- nett, by post 1/2.*

BREEDERS' AND EXHIBITORS' RECORD,
For the Registration of Particulars concerning Pedigree Stock of every Description. By W. K. TAUNTON. In three parts. *In cloth, price each 2/6 nett, or the set 6/- nett, by post 6/6.*
Part I., The Pedigree Record. Part II., The Stud Record.
Part III., The Show Record.

B. & S.'s
DOG MEDICINES,

As Used by the Leading Dog Breeders and Fanciers.

DISTEMPER PILLS (B. & S.'s).—These valuable Pills are a certain cure for this most destructive disease; if given immediately on the appearance of the first symptoms, and have proved the means of saving the lives of innumerable Dogs of all Breeds.

WORM POWDERS (B. & S.'s) are admitted, by all who have tried them, to be the best, cheapest, and most speedy Medicine for the removal of all the varieties of Intestinal Worms, from which the Canine race is so peculiarly liable to suffer.

ALTERATIVE POWDERS (B. & S.'s).—We can strongly recommend these Powders to Dog Owners as an infallible cure for Constipation, Liver Complaints, Indigestion, &c., and as a *safe* and *reliable Laxative*. Being tasteless, the Powders can be given to any dog in a little bread and milk, or its ordinary food, so that the trouble and danger of administering "Pills" or "Balls" are entirely obviated. The "Alterative Powders" in consequence of their great effect as a Cooling and Blood-Purifying Medicine are particularly useful in all cases of skin disease.

TONIC PILLS (B. & S.'s).—Unrivalled for Dogs recovering from Distemper and other debilitating diseases, as they not only improve the appetite, but also strengthen the Digestive Organs and the system generally.

COUGH PILLS (B. & S.'s).—These should be given immediately on the appearance of Coughs or Colds, and will be found to effect a speedy and permanent cure.

PALATABLE PUPPY POWDERS (B. & S.'s).—Almost tasteless and can be administered in a small quantity of bread and milk. Given occasionally up to 12 months old they act as a preventative of Distemper, Worms, and Convulsions—the sources of 99 per cent. of puppy mortality.

☛ The above Medicines are all retailed in Boxes from 1s. (or Post Free, 1s. 1½d.) upwards, and prepared in four different strengths, called respectively A, B, C, & D.
 A Strength is suitable for St. Bernards, Boarhounds, &c.
 B   „   „   Foxhounds, Retrievers, Greyhounds, &c.
 C   „   „   Fox Terriers, Dachshunds, &c.
 D   „   „   The smaller breeds of Dogs.

MANGE WASH (B. & S.'s).—An infallible Remedy for every variety of this most troublesome disease. (N.B.—The curative action of this Wash is greatly facilitated by the use of the Aperient Balls.) 1s. 9d. per bottle (or Post Free, 2s. 3d.).

EAR CANKER DROPS (B. & S.'s).—A specific for this painful and troublesome complaint. 1s. per bottle (or Post Free, 1s. 3d.).

CANINE ECZEMA OINTMENT (B. & S.'s).—This has been used with *marvellous success* in many *very bad cases* of this troublesome Canine complaint. In pots, 1s. (Post Free, 1s. 3d.) and 2s. 6d (Post Free, 2s. 9d.) each.

CHAMPION DOG SOAP (B. & S.'s) will be found unequalled for Cleansing and Purifying the Skin, whilst it entirely removes all objectionable smell and every description of Insect Life. In tablets 6d. (Post Free, 7½d.) and 1s. (Post Free, 1s. 1d.).

N.B.—Complete Lists, and advice as to use of these Remedies, gratis.

SPECIMEN TESTIMONIAL.

Mrs. White, Park Horner Farm, Wimborne, Dorset, writes :   October 24th, 1908.
 "I recommend these [B. & S.'s Palatable Puppy Powders] Powders which *I have used for some years, and I have never had a pup yet to have Distemper*, therefore I have great faith in them."

A correspondent writing in the BAZAAR of April 23rd, 1909, says :—
 "I have lately been trying the 'Champion Dog Soap' sent out by Bird & Storey. It is a capital cleanser, does not irritate the skin, and takes little or nothing out of the jacket of a hard-coated variety, like the fox terrier, for instance. This is a point which should not be lost sight of by fanciers . . . 'Champion Dog Soap' lathers freely, and thus is a labour-saver, another point in its favour . . . Those who go in for showing dogs will find it a capital soap to use."

BIRD & STOREY, Canine Chemists,
42, CASTLE STREET EAST, OXFORD STREET, LONDON, W.

Advice] **ESTABLISHED 1850.** [Gratis.

DOGS—RACKHAM'S DISTEMPER BALLS. The only cure for Distemper known, no matter at what stage. Have been used in the principal kennels for 50 years. Price 1/-, 2/6, 5/-, 10/-, 20/-; free 2d. extra.

DOGS—RACKHAM'S JAPANESE WORM BALLS. One dose sufficient. No other medicine required. Price 1/-, 2/6, 5/-, 10/-, 20/-; free 2d. extra.

DOGS—RACKHAM'S KATALEPRA. Cures Red Mange, Eczema, and all Skin Diseases. Price 1/-, 2/6, 5/-, 10/-, 20/-; free 2d. extra.

DOGS—RACKHAM'S TONIC CONDITION BALLS are invaluable for Greyhounds and Whippets in Training, Sporting, Exhibition or Stud Dogs, also for ailing and delicate Pups. Brings them into the highest state of condition and health. Price 1/-, 2/6, 5/-, 10/-, 20/-; free 2d. extra.

DOGS—RACKHAM'S ANTI-DISTEMPER SPECIFIC. Prevents contagion at shows; Cures Distemper; no loss of Appetite; with Toy Dogs and small Puppies its effects are marvellous. Price 1/-, 2/6, 5/-, 10/-, 20/-.

DOGS—RACKHAM'S EAR CANKER SPECIFIC. Cures both internal and external Canker. Price 1/-, 2/6, 5/-; free 2d. extra.

DOGS—RACKHAM'S JAPAN SOAP. For washing Dogs. Kills all Vermin; removes itching and odour; prevents Red Mange and Eczema. Cleanses, disinfects and beautifies. Tablets, 6d. and 1/-. Post free 8 or 15 stamps.

DOGS—RACKHAM'S PUPPY WORM BALLS. For Puppies of all breeds and Toy Dogs. A new remedy. We have introduced this preparation in a most convenient form. They are perfectly safe to give, and will be found most efficacious. Therefore, why let your Puppies die from worms? Price 1/-, 2/6, 5/-, 10/-, 20/-; post free 2d. extra.

DOGS—RACKHAM'S DACTYLA PUPPY FOOD. For Pups after weaning. Is thoroughly cooked; contains our Meat Powder and Fruit Food; prevents Worms and Rickets. This is a perfect food; is also invaluable for dogs suffering or recovering from disease. Price 21/- cwt., 10/6 ½cwt., 5/3 ¼cwt.

DOGS—RACKHAM'S IMPROVED DOG BRUSHES. Suitable for all breeds of dogs. They are the best made and cheapest brushes. Prices 2/3, 2/6, 3/-; post free. Pet Dog Brush, 1/9, 2/3, 3/3; post free. Special for Yorkshire Terriers.

DOGS — RACKHAM'S JAPANESE WORM POWDERS. A tasteless and most certain remedy. "One dose sufficient." They are also a splendid alterative medicine for all dogs. Price 1/-, 2/6, 5/-, 10/-, 20/-; free 2d. extra.

DOGS—RACKHAM'S DACTYLA, THE NEW FOOD FOR DOGS. Contains our Dried Meat Powder—also a scientifically prepared admixture of dates and other Eastern fruits. Keeps system and skin cool, healthy, and coat glossy. Price 19/6 cwt., 9/9 ½cwt., 5/- ¼ cwt.

DOGS—RACKHAM'S GREYHOUND BISCUITS. For Greyhounds and Whippets in training. The very best food for keeping dogs healthy, vigorous, agile, and fit for any work. Price 21/- cwt., 10/6 ½cwt.

DOGS—RACKHAM'S NORFOLK HOUNDMEAL. A splendid food for all Dogs, especially aged dogs. Contains our Meat Powder, Supplied in small or large grades. Price 16/- per cwt., 8/- ½cwt., 4/- ¼cwt.

RACKHAM & CO., St. Peter's, Norwich.

Kennel Indispensables.

The Ideal Disinfectant

Famous as a cure for Mange, Eczema, Ringworm, and all other parasitic skin diseases.

A GRAND HAIR PRODUCER.

Destroys all insects such as fleas, lice, ticks, etc.
Sold in tins at 9d., 1/3, 2/- each; 6/- per gallon.
Free for P.O.

The Kennel, the Stable, the Poultry Yard kept sweet and healthy.
Ask for IZAL Veterinary Pamphlet.

IZAL Disinfectant Powder.

THE STRONGEST POWDER KNOWN.

In tins, 6d. and 1/- each; 50 lb. casks, 5/-. Free for P.O.

IZAL Soft Soap, *8d. per lb. Post free.*
IZAL Bar Soap. *8d. per lb. Post free.*

Special quotations for large lots.

NEWTON, CHAMBERS & Co., Ltd.,
THORNCLIFFE, NEAR SHEFFIELD.

BARNARDS LIMITED, NORWICH

IMPROVED RANGE OF KENNELS AND RUNS.
No. 347.

Each kennel, 6ft. wide, 5ft. deep. Runs, each 6ft. long, 6ft. wide, finished in the very best style.

One House and Run	£7	10	0
Two Houses and Runs	12	15	0
Three ditto	18	18	0
Six ditto	35	0	0

Carriage Paid.

NEW PORTABLE KENNEL AND RUN.
Registered Design.
No. 345.

3ft. 6in. wide, 8ft. long, 4ft. high	£4	5	0
4ft. wide, 9ft. 6in. long, 5ft. high	5	10	0
5ft. wide, 12ft. long, 5ft. high	7	10	0

Carriage Paid.

IMPROVED KENNEL.
No. 348.

AWARDED GOLD MEDAL SCHEVENINGEN, 1901 and 1906.

For Terriers	£1	7	6
For Collies, &c.	2	5	6
For Mastiffs	3	9	6

Carriage Paid.

LEAN-TO PORTABLE KENNEL AND RUN.
No. 346

House, 4ft. by 3ft. 6in. Run, 4ft. by 6ft.

Cash Price **£5 0 0**
Wood Back for Run, **22/6** extra.
Corrugated Iron round Run ... ... **5/-** extra.
Reversible Trough **5/-**

Carriage Paid.

CATALOGUE FREE:
Norfolk Iron Works, Norwich.

Lightning Source UK Ltd.
Milton Keynes UK
UKHW01f1001110618
324047UK00001B/57/P